CONTENTS

INTRODUCTION AND SUMMARY

This report has been commissioned by IPPR as part of a wider project to develop strategies for a modern welfare system. The project is based on the premise that the key to a just and flourishing society is that everyone should have an equal chance in life, but that people do not start out as equals: it is therefore necessary to redistribute some of society's goods in order to eliminate avoidable disadvantage, or to compensate where disadvantage is unavoidable. The purpose of a welfare system is to ensure that, as far as possible, everyone is able to participate in society, to enjoy its fruits and to realise their own potential.

Childcare makes a major contribution to the relief of disadvantage and to the promotion of equality. And since these goals are central, childcare should be seen not as an adjunct or afterthought, but as a key component of a modern welfare system.

The value of childcare as a strategy for welfare has several dimensions. It has a vital role to play not only in meeting children's needs, but also in enabling adults to combine the responsibilities of parenthood with paid employment. It is especially important in helping mothers to achieve financial independence, which is one of the surest ways of protecting families from the hardship associated with lone parenthood, divorce and widowhood. At the same time, it is a central factor in enabling women to be educated, trained, employed and paid on an equal footing with men.

Because of its impact on women's earning power and family income, providing childcare is one of the most effective ways of relieving child poverty. Furthermore, there is evidence from longitudinal studies that children fare better if they have pre-school experience of group childare: they do better at school, they are less likely to get into trouble with the law, and they are more likely to get jobs. Childcare services for school-age children help prevent accidents, vandalism and crime.

There is an overwhelming case for childcare being a matter of public responsibility. That is not to say that it is for government alone: families, employers, trade unions and communities have a part to play. However, government should take a strong lead, setting out a national childcare policy with clear objectives - and making sure that it is implemented.

Childcare in a Modern Welfare System

Towards a new national policy

Bronwen Cohen and Neil Fraser

ACKNOWLEDGEMENTS

The authors wish to thank the following for their help in preparing this report: Heather Joshi, Jane Millar, Peter Moss, Henry Neuberger, Helen Penn, Jo Roll, Gill Scott, Robin Simpson, Adrian Sinfield, Holly Sutherland, Jenny Williams, Marion Kosak, Anne Longfield; none is responsible for the outcome. Thanks also to the Joseph Rowntree Foundation for funding this research; to the TSB Group, who supported the seminar at which policy options were discussed and helped to fund the publication of the report; and to all those who attended the seminar. Special thanks are due to Anna Coote and Polly Pattullo for their substantial work in editing the final report.

THE AUTHORS

Bronwen Cohen is Director of the Scottish Childcare and Family Alliance and UK Expert for the European Commission's Childcare Network. She is the author of several books and papers on childcare in the UK and Europe.

Neil Fraser is an economist and senior lecturer in the Social Policy Department at the University of Edinburgh. He is co-author of *The Real Cost of Unemployment*, BBC, 1985.

Such a policy should have a comprehensive approach, which understands that childcare has many functions and must serve a range of interests.

- Childcare is for parents, whether they are employed, in education or training, or not employed.
- Childcare is for all children, pre-school and school-age; it must also meet the distinctive requirements of children in disadvantaged urban areas and in rural areas, those from ethnic and linguistic minorities, and those with special needs.
- Childcare is for society: it is part of the social and economic infrastructure of a thriving community.

Although the main objective of childcare as part of a modern welfare system is to promote greater equality in terms of life chances, it it also an important welfare goal to give people greater autonomy and more control over their own lives. Individuals have widely varying requirements and public provision must be sufficiently responsive to meet the need for childcare in a diversity of ways.

This report demonstrates that current provision of childcare is woefully inadequate. The new emphasis placed by the 1989 Children Act on local authorities' duty to protect children 'in need' perpetuates the narrow focus of public responsibility, which threatens to reduce public childcare to a disadvantaged and stigmatised ghetto.

The report explores the impact of childcare (or lack of it) - on women, children and men, and on the social and economic life of the community. It sets provision in the UK in the context of policy and practice in the European Community, showing how far the UK lags behind. Unlike most of its EC partners, the UK has no national policy, but merely a jumble of fragmented, inconsistent and often poor-quality services, developed on an ad hoc basis. The report suggests that the UK is missing oportunities to use EC funds to help provide more childcare places.

It sets out guiding principles for a national childcare policy:

- Childcare is a key component of a modern welfare system
- Childcare must serve a range of interests: parents, children and society.

- Provision must be equitable and responsive.
- Provision must seek to integrate education and care.
- Policies on childcare must be linked with improved provision for employed parents.

The report explores strategic options for public support of childcare, in the light of the principles outlined above: which strategies are more likely to serve the objectives of a national childcare policy? It compares the advantages and disadvantages of demand subsidies such as tax relief and 'childcare vouchers' with those of supply subsidies, including public provision of childcare and public funding of provision by non-government organisations; it considers the case for funding for-profit as well as not-for profit services. It concludes:

- Public provision is most likely to meet the need for volume services, but this is not sufficient on its own, because it cannot meet the full range of needs for childcare.
- Public funding of non-government providers should concentrate on supporting not-for-profit organisations, through capital and operational grants, and through support for training. This should seek to build on their proven strengths: for innovation and experiment, for enabling communities to take action on their own behalf and set up services to suit their own preferences, for meeting minority needs and for identifying gaps in public services.
- Public support to the for-profit sector should be through training for care workers.
- Government should bear the full costs of the educational element of childcare, and arguably also 70 per cent of the care element. There should be greater public support for services for the under threes. Greater efforts should be made to obtain financial support from the European structural funds, for childcare in some parts of the UK. Public funding of childcare should be regarded as a sound financial investment.
- Thirty per cent of the care element of childcare should be borne by parents. A system of fee relief should be introduced to help lower-income families. This will mean that some parents will pay more than 30 per cent and others less, or nothing at all.

- Employers should be encouraged to enter into partnership arrangements with local authorities and other interested organisations, to provide childcare. They should be obliged by law to improve provisions for working parents. But there should be no compulsory levy on employers to pay for childcare.

The report argues that government has a key role to play in ensuring that childcare services are consistent with national policy. This entails understanding and responding to local needs; setting standards and measuring performance; promoting parental choice; training childcare workers; promoting good employment practices; regular review and inspection. The reports sets out examples of best practice in the UK and other European countries.

It proposes priorities for government.

Central government:

- give a strong political direction, with responsibility invested in a cabinet-level minister; the best option is likely to be the Department of Eduation and Science;
- publish clear objectives;
- make full provision for research and assessment;
- set aside funds to be administered through local authorities;
- amend the Children Act to extend the duty of local authorities to review the childcare needs of all children.

Local government:

- develop a co-ordinated childcare strategy, with one department giving strong leadership;
- audit local childcare needs and current provision;
- publish clear objectives in line with national policy, adapted to local needs and conditions;
- make the most of existing resources: increase direct provision; fund non-government providers; develop grant-aid strategies to help communities set up services themselves, to meet their own needs;

- open dialogue with local employers, colleges and other interested organisations and pursue partnership arrangements where possible;
- set standards and measure performance to ensure that provision is in line with national and local objectives.

The cost-benefit analysis in Part Two estimates that of three million children living below the poverty line, about 1.25 million are under five: of these, up to half could be brought out of poverty if childcare enabled their mothers to work. It is likely that many more would be brought out of poverty if childcare services were developed alongside a reform of tax and benefit systems, to remove disincentives caused by the 'povery trap', which especially affect lone parents and mothers living with unemployed men. These policies are considered in more detail in a forthcoming IPPR publication (Bransbury).

This report argues that childcare can play a major part in increasing the supply of labour and skills, combatting underlying inflationary pressures and helping to gavalanise the economy. It demonstrates that public investment in childcare pays dividends – by improving the social well-being of families and communities and by bringing substantial medium and long-term financial gains to households and to the Treasury.

Anna Coote
Series Editor

ORIGINS OF PUBLIC CHILDCARE

In 1816, Robert Owen opened a nursery for the children of his employees in the mill town of New Lanark in Scotland. The nursery was to be a play area for children 'from the time they can walk alone until they enter school' and a demonstration of Owen's own progressive educational theories. At the same time, it met the practical needs of parents working at his factory. In 1813, Owen wrote:

> The parents will be relieved from the loss of time and from the care and anxiety which are now occasioned by attendance on their children from the period when they can go alone to that at which they enter the school. The child will be placed in a situation of safety, where with its future schoolfellows and companions it will acquire the best habits and principles, while at meal times and at night it will return to the caresses of its parents and the affections of each are likely to be increased by the separation.

Owen was also aware of the needs of school age chidren. He noted in the same essay:

> The area is also to be a place of meeting for the children from five to ten years of age, previous to and after school hours. (Owen,1813)

Owen's school took 600 children from the age of 18 months up to 10 or sometimes 12 years, and young people for evening classes. It was open from 7.30 am to 5 pm with two breaks. The infant school was free. Classes for older children occupied half the time, and for the rest of the time the children were 'allowed to amuse themselves at perfect freedom in a large paved area in front of the Institute with the younger children' (Owen,1972).

In Owen's Institute – developed as a model for society – the functions of care and education were linked and integral to the extensive welfare programme developed for his employees. Care and education of young children would later develop into separate spheres, but the dual emphasis – which in the second half of the 20th century became known as 'educare' – was not uncommon in the first half of the 19th century.

The first nurseries were established by enlightened employers and charities worried by the quality of the childcare, usually 'day nursing' or childminding, organised by the women factory workers for their children. Increasing interest in the benefits of education, led in a number of countries to these early nurseries providing both care and education. In France, for example, children's 'shelters' were established in the 1840s to provide care and education for children from the age of two to six or seven; originally opened for 12 hours a day, they ultimately became nursery schools under the Ministry of Education. In Germany and Belgium, private (voluntary) organisations developed provision in the early 19th century for working-class families. In Belgium, government funding was made available in 1842, developing from a simple safeguarding role to more educationally based provision, financed by the Belgium Ministry of Education. (Moss, 1989)

The first public involvement in the United Kingdom in the provision of day nurseries was triggered by the 1914-1918 war when over 100 day nurseries were set up across the country. At the end of the war, local health authorities were enpowered by law to provide day nurseries or to assist voluntary nurseries. By this time, pre-school educational provision had begun its separate development. Schools established under the 1870 Education Act took in a considerable number of children from the two to five age group. By 1901, 43 per cent of three year olds in England and Wales were on elementary school registers. However, following a recommendation in 1905 by the inspectorate that children under five should be excluded, this dropped by 1919 to 17 per cent. (Summerfield)

The 1918 Education Act allowed local authorities to establish nursery schools but neither health nor education legislation led to extensive provision. By 1938, for example, there were only 4000 places in public nurseries and just over 9500 in nursery education. Once again, war prompted a change of direction. The second world war encouraged women's employment and so women were helped with childcare. The initiative came from the Ministry of Labour which proposed not just more extensive childcare, but also help for women such as shopping leave, factory canteens, an expanded school-meal service and part-time work. By the end of the war there were nursery places for 62,000 children in England and Wales, more than double the number of places available in 1988, with similar programmes in Scotland and Northern Ireland.

However, the nurseries began to be closed even before the end of the war and within 20 years only a third remained open. The closures reflected the view that women would and should withdraw from the workforce when wartime needs disappeared. This view was reinforced by post-war child-rearing theory emphasising the dangers of early separation of mother and child and favouring, where care was necessary, individual rather than group care.

This attitude was fundamental to the welfare reforms of the early post-war period which defined women principally as dependants of men. The reforms went some way to recognising the direct costs of children through the introduction of a tax-financed family allowance system for all families with two or more children. Together, with child tax allowances, this provided the basis of financial support for families until the introduction of Child Benefit in 1975. However, the lack of recognition of women's economic role meant that childcare needs and work and family issues were excluded from the scope of welfare reform. In particular, the reforms did not anticipate the increasing impact upon families of the indirect costs of children from the loss or reduction of maternal income. For women did not abandon work on marriage. Between 1940 and 1944, 62 per cent of women had worked between marriage and the birth of their first child, rising to 88 per cent of those with a birth between 1975 and 1979. (Martin and Roberts).

Maternal employment began to rise from the late 1950s, but government policies continued to reflect the view that a child should be the mother's responsibility. A Ministry of Health circular in 1968, for example, recommended that priority for public nursery places should be given to children either with only one parent 'who has no option but to go out to work' or those with health or welfare needs. (This policy was continued by the Department of Health and Social Security which took over responsibility in 1970 from the Ministry of Health.)

The 1944 Education Act had made provision for nursery education through a duty on local authorities (made discretionary in 1980), but nursery education did not increase significantly until after the 1967 Plowden Report on primary education – and then largely on a part-time basis. Plowden had recommended part-time provision because of 'the dangers of allowing children to attend a nursery school or class at too early an age for too long a period each day.' Ironically, until 1980 there were more three and four year olds within infant classes of primary schools (in general, in larger classes and with a less appropriate curriculum than in nursery education) than there were in nursery education.

The rationing of local authority day nursery places contributed, at first implicitly, and then explicitly, to a restrictive definition of the local authority's role as provider of childcare services. The 1989 Children Act confirmed the role of local authorities in providing a range of services for children 'in need', while government ministers have continued to emphasise that if working parents wanted care they should find and pay for it themselves (see below, p.9). Most recently the Government has suggested that employers have responsibilities in this area.

At the same time, a steady growth in other services, in particular less formal services, has enhanced the role of local authorities as regulators. A substantial increase in childminding occurred as mothers remained in, or returned to, paid employment and education. The number of places with registered childminders in England and Wales increased from 1700 in 1949 to 47,200 in 1968. Childminding regulations were extended in 1968: local authorities were empowered to provide more support for childminders and registration requirements were tightened. However, as Joan Lestor, the Labour minister, indicated at the time, childminders were not to be seen as the ultimate solution to the problems of childcare:

> The ultimate object of any solution to the problems of the under fives is obviously an urgent expansion of the day nursery service. (Mayall and Petrie)

Although local authorities now make more direct use of childminders to meet some of their statutory duties, there are only occasional examples of publicly provided or extensively supported childminding services in the UK, unlike some other European Commission countries. In Denmark, for example, publicly employed childminders now care for over twice as many children as private childminders. (Langstad and Sommer). The UK's longest standing salaried minders' scheme, started in Battersea, south London, in 1975, lost its funding in 1988.

The local authority's role as regulator rather than as provider has been enlarged further since the mid-1960s by the growth of the playgroup movement. Playgroups, first started by women who recognised the need for their children to play in the company of other children, now provide more places than nursery education although on an even more restricted basis. Average weekly attendance in playgroups in 1988 was two to three sessions per child. Playgroups have evolved from a 'stop-gap' measure and now see themselves as an alternative to publicly provided nursery education. In its 1989 Statement of Principles, the Pre-School Playgroups Association in England emphasised that playgroups 'are a major provider of pre-school education ...(with) an equal role to play with other agencies in national and local strategies for pre-school provision' (Statham et al)

Government policy towards playgroups has evolved in a similar manner and they are seen as providing 'diversity' and 'choice'. However, an uneven distribution of services (described below, p.18) renders parental choice frequently illusory, but playgroups have been used by some local authorities as an alternative to nursery education. The low public cost of this form of provision undoubtedly contributed to its rapid expansion.

The most recent extension in the regulating role of local authorities has come from a rapid increase in private nurseries, particularly in more affluent areas. This change, together with a reduction in some local authority provision, has meant that private and voluntary nurseries now provide more places than local authority nurseries. The increase has found some authorities ill-prepared and many more under resourced for coping with this role of registering and regulating private nurseries. A recent small-scale study of the private nursery sector found local authority staff often uncertain of their powers in registering and monitoring provision and 'ambivalent or resentful' about the time they were having to spend on the private nurseries. (Penn)

The limited public involvement in the provision of services has been paralleled over the same period by limited statutory work and family employment provisions. Maternity provisions were introduced in 1975 but were only made available subject to stringent qualifying conditions which exclude many women. A further right to paid time off for ante-natal care for all pregnant women was introduced by the Conservative Government in 1980, but since then no further provision has been introduced. Changes further restricting access to maternity rights were proposed in 1986 in a Government White Paper, Building Businesses not Barriers, but not implemented. However, the thinking behind the White Paper suggests that there will be no new provision. Indeed, the Government has opposed the European Commission's initiatives (see below, p.43), most notably parental and family leave and a recent proposal which would have given all employed pregnant women 14 weeks' fully paid maternity leave.

A changing demography

The UK has 10.7 million children under the age of 15. More than three and a half million of these are under five (OPCS, 1988). The total number of children under 15 has fallen for two decades but is projected to increase up to the end of the century when it will start to fall again. The number of under fives is also increasing, but is expected to fall again from the mid-1990s.

Decline of European fertility rates

Women throughout Europe are having their families later and having fewer children. In the UK, the average age for a woman to have her first child has risen to 25 while between 1970 and 1987 the number of children per woman dropped from 2.44 to 1.82 (IPPR Social Policy Paper No.1, Coote et al, 1990). One result of this long-term decline has been the reduction in the number of school leavers and a recognition of the need to increase female employment. The rest of the Community countries have experienced an even greater decline in fertility rates: in Italy and the Federal Republic of Germany, the rate in 1988 was 1.33 and 1.40 respectively while in the Netherlands, Portugal, Denmark, Spain and Greece it was 1.56 or less. (CEC 1990b)

Many European children are now growing up within smaller families with fewer opportunities for play within the family. In 1985, except in Ireland and Italy, of households with a child under ten more than half contained just one child; only 10 per cent or less had three or more young children. (Moss, 1988)

The increase in the numbers of cohabiting couples and divorced people remarrying has changed the shape of households. While the majority of children continue to live with both natural parents, an increasing proportion has some experience outside nuclear family settings. The number of one-parent families has increased from 6 per cent of households with dependent children in 1961 to 13 per cent in 1987 (Sorrentino). This is largely due to the increase in divorce rates (six-fold between 1960 and 1986) but also to a growing number of never married mothers. Between 1960 and 1986, births to unmarried women increased as a percentage of live births from 5 per cent to 21 per cent. In 1986, 29 per cent of these births were to teenage mothers, creating childcare needs in relation to schooling as well as employment or further education (Sorrentino). This is also a European trend, even in those countries such as Italy where numbers are currently low.(CECb)

Such developments highlight the failure of the welfare system to take adequate account of the economic role of women. Family poverty, as we shall see, is closely linked to lone parenthood and, more particularly, lone motherhood.

More mothers at work

There has been an increase in women's employment in all European countries including the UK, and more and more this involves mothers of dependent children. UK women's overall participation rates are high but until recently employment rates for mothers of under fives have been extremely low. Over the last few years these have increased significantly – from 29 per cent in 1985 to 37 per cent in 1988. However, the rate of full time employment remains the second lowest in Europe (see below, p.48) and the rate of full time employment amongst lone mothers with a child under five is the lowest. (Cohen, 1990)

Paying attention to trends

Throughout Europe and the developed world these employment trends have contributed to a strong and rising demand for daycare. At the same time, other trends, such as smaller families, a growing awareness of children's physical and social well-being and a greater understanding of the benefits of high quality pre-school services, are placing additional demands on childcare services. These changes have prompted reviews of childcare provision – in the 1960s and 1970s in countries such as Sweden, Denmark and Italy; and more recently in Canada, the United States, Australia and New Zealand. Nothing similar has happened in the UK.

As we see in the next chapter, the UK retains an infrastructure and level of childcare provision that is inadequate to meet either the demand for childcare or the nature of family and employment patterns. The place of childcare in the country's welfare and education system is yet to be established.

PATTERNS OF PROVISION

Childcare services broadly comprise care for parents in paid employment, education and training, care to meet 'welfare' and social needs of children and families, educational and play services and care for short periods. There is, however, not always a clear distinction between the functions of each type of service: for example, most service providers for under fives would see themselves as concerned in some way with stimulating learning and development. Similarly, education and play services are used by parents to provide care.

Services are widely considered to have developed in an unnecessarily fragmented form: there has, for example, been little attempt to encourage functional integration of services where appropriate, in particular in relation to education and care; nor indeed has there been a coherent approach in relation to policy.

Government policy over the past decade has emphasised the responsibility of parents (and more recently employers) to find and pay for daycare except when children and families are in particular need of provision, on the grounds of welfare. Over the years, successive government ministers have specifically rejected the concept of any public responsibility in ensuring the availability of daycare for working parents.

> Daycare will continue to be primarily a matter of private arrangement between parents and private and voluntary resources except when there are special needs . . . (John Patten, Hansard, March 18, 1985).
>
> Our view is that it is for parents that go out to work to decide how best to care for their children. If they want to or need help in this they should make the appropriate arrangements and meet the costs. (Edwina Currie, Hansard, July 12, 1988).
>
> If you have to work you do and if you have to find childcare you find it. When I say 'have' I mean if you really want to. (Angela Rumbold, Family Policy Bulletin, March 1991).

Access to many services which provide daycare is therefore determined by ability to pay. This contributes to social differences in the use of the range of provision.

Who provides?

The principal funding providers are local authorities, some education and public bodies, voluntary organisations, employers, and, overwhelmingly, parents, relatives and friends (both as direct providers and through self-help voluntary services). These are all providers as well as funders (for example, relatives fund care with their time), although they may not themselves directly provide the services. Other providers are private companies, nannies and childminders.

Local authorities are the most extensive funding providers for education services, but as providers of daycare they have become far less significant than private nurseries. Local authority day nurseries are non-existent in some areas. However, the role of local authorities as funders of other services - for example, using childminders for some welfare placements or for funding voluntary agency services - has increased in recent years.

Voluntary providers range from the larger child-based charities, largely concerned with meeting welfare needs, to smaller local services developed by parents and/or others within the community.

Employer providers include those running their own nurseries, those involved in partnership nurseries which may involve a charitable structure, and those using private companies or individuals to provide the service on their behalf.

Parents are the most extensive providers of care including daycare (half of women working part time and 13 per cent of women working full time use husbands to care for their children, Martin and Roberts, 1984). Parents also contribute extensively to self-help services such as playgroups. Grandparents (in particular, maternal grandparents), aunts and uncles, older siblings, friends and neighbours are also used to provide daycare.

Private providers range from self employed childminders and nannies, and small private nurseries to large commercial companies.

What is provided?

Daycare services for under fives

Day nurseries

Provide full and/or part-time daycare for under fives usually from

8am-6pm for a miniumum of 50 weeks in the year. May be run by local authorities, employers, education and training establishments, voluntary organisations or community groups or privately. Local authority provision is low cost or free to parents. Voluntary and employer provision variable. Private provision full cost.

Most local authority provision is restricted to families with social or health needs. A small number of local authorities offer combined care and education within 'combined centres'. Family centres are a further variant of local authority nurseries. Some, but not all of these, offer part- or full-time daycare as one of a number of services. Some offer a wider range of activities to the community. The most recent variant by a small but growing number of local authorities is partnership provision involving a range of strategies for developing nursery provision in partnership with employers, development agencies and voluntary providers.

Some day nurseries are run by voluntary organisations and community groups. Charities are now more involved in developing innovative approaches to meet the wider needs of disadvantaged families. However, some are again beginning to become involved in the provision of daycare in recognition of its role in combatting poverty.

Community nurseries started to appear in London during the 1970s, often set up by frustrated parents unable to find daycare, and their development was fostered through generous funding from the Greater London Council. Some community nurseries were set up by black parents specifically to meet the linguistic and broader cultural needs of black children.

A small number of nurseries are provided by employers for their employees. An Industrial Relations Review and Report survey in 1989 found that three per cent of employers assisted with childcare. Since the survey was of their subscribers - and so likely to offer above average employment conditions - this figure over-represents the proportion providing assistance. Sometimes, employer-provided nurseries are run directly by employees, sometimes by commercial firms. Partnership arrangements with other employers or other partners including local authorities and education and training organisations are increasingly common.

The private sector is now (with the voluntary sector) the biggest provider of day nursery places. Providers range from small nurseries which have, in some cases, developed from an extended childminding arrangement to nursery 'chains'. Some private nurseries are registered as day nurseries but are described as nursery schools and may in some cases have a more explicitly educational content.

Childminders

> Provide full and/or part-time daycare usually from 8am-6pm for a minimum of 50 weeks of the year in their own homes for under fives and school age childcare for over fives. In general UK childminders are self-employed. Local authority sponsored places free or low cost. Otherwise full cost.

Childminders must register with their local social services department although as many as one in five (or more) are thought not to be registered. Childminders are required, in general, to care for no more than three children under five including their own, and where a childminder works with another childminder or an assistant in a quasi-nursery, new draft guidance suggests a ratio of 2:7. Childminders are generally poorly supported. The National Childminding Association reports long waiting-lists for registration and a failure of many local authorities to maintain adequate monitoring. Local authorities make increasing use of sponsored childminders to meet their statutory obligations to children 'in need'.

Nannies

> Provide care in the parents' own home for under fives and over fives to meet parental hours requirements. May be shared between families. Full cost.

Some nannies live with the family, some work on a daily basis. They are employees of the family but their status is not always clear and some may not have a contract of employment. Some families now use a shared nanny arrangement - in which one nanny looks after the children of two or more families. Nannies are excluded from regulation and control except when employed by more than two sets of parents when they have to be registered under the new Children Act.

Care for parents in education and training

Some education and training organisations run their own day nurseries. Some offer full daycare, although in some colleges provision is sometimes more restricted, involving a playgroup for older pre-school children for more limited periods of time. Some creches are available and there are a few isolated examples of facilities for mothers still at school.

Table 2.1: Daycare services for under fives, 1985 and 1988

	1985 No. of places	Places as % of population, aged 0-4	1988 No. of places	Places as % of population aged 0-4	
Local authority day nurseries	32,964	0.9	34,225	0.9	Publicly provided and funded
Private and voluntary day nurseries	27,533	0.8	40,378	1.1	Publicly regulated. Limited public funding through voluntary grants and limited tax concessions
Registered childminders	144,908	4.0	189,054	5.0	Publicly regulated. Isolated examples of public provision. Limited public funding of some sponsored places and hiring
Nannies (1985 estimate)	30,000		30,000		Non-regulated except where shared by more than two families
Total	235,405	6.5	293,657	7.8	

Source: Cohen (1990)

Table 2.1 provides a summary of the levels of provision within daycare services. Statistics are incomplete and do not, for example, distinguish between different forms of day nurseries. Statistics in relation to local authority provision do not separate out day nurseries, combined centres or family centres and do not take account of the fact that nurseries may not now be providing daycare. Similarly private and voluntary providers are grouped together and there are no statistics on the number of employer provided nurseries. There are no statistics at all for unregulated areas of provision.

Who gets daycare

Table 2.1 shows that in 1988 (including the 1985 estimate for nannies) there were a total of 293,657 daycare places. This means there were places for nearly eight per cent of under fives. Publicly provided services - in the form of local authority nurseries - account at most for 11 per cent of total daycare provision. The number of daycare places increased between 1985-1988 largely as a result of an increase in the number of registered childminders and private nursery provision. Despite these increases there are still only day nursery places for approximately two per cent of under fives and daycare provision for less than eight per cent of under fives. Private and voluntary day nurseries are for the first time now providing more places than publicly funded day nurseries. While voluntary provision plays an important role in ensuring that most children have some access to pre-school provision, grants to the voluntary sector in England and Wales in 1987-88 totalled less than £2 million.

Education services for under fives

Nursery schools and classes

> Provide education, most often part-time for mainly three to four year olds. Half-day sessions vary from two to two and a half hours, for 40 weeks of the year. In general provided by local education authorities, but a small and increasing proportion of places are within private schools. Local education authority (LEA) provision free.

The principal providers are LEAs who are empowerered but not now required to provide nursery education for children aged two to five. Most LEAs do make some provision in the form of nursery schools or more often, nursery classes.

Primary schools

> Provide education through early admission policies, usually full-time for six to six and a half hours a day 40 weeks of the year for mainly four year olds. Principal providers are local education authorities whose provision is free. A small number of places are provided by LEAs and voluntary agencies for children with special needs. Some private schools may have early admission policies.

Children are required to start school from five with the exception of Northern Ireland where the age of compulsory schooling has been lowered to four. Many local education authorities have early admissions policies, some involving admitting children to school at the beginning of the year when they are five, some at the beginning of the term in which they are five. 1986 survey evidence found that few authorities adjusted their pupil-teacher ratio to take account of the younger children within the reception classes.

Who gets nursery education

Table 2.2: Education services for under fives UK, 1988

	No. of full-time places	No. of part-time places	Total places	Places as % of population, aged 3-4	
LEA nursery schools and classes	56,696	302,614	359,310	25	Publicly provided
LEA primary schools	275,530	21,552	297,082	20	Publicly provided
LEA special schools			6,000	0.4	Publicly provided
Independent schools			40,000	2.7	Limited public funding through voluntary grants and tax concessions

Source: Cohen (1990)

Table 2.2 and 2.3 show that one quarter of the UK's three and four year olds are now in nursery education, the proportion having risen only slightly between 1985-1988. The overwhelming majority (84 per cent) of these places are part-time and there are full-time equivalent places for only 14 per cent of three and four year olds. One in five of three and four year olds are in local education authority primary schools which may not have the appropriate staffing and curriculum for children of this age. This proportion has not increased, but as with nursery education, the number of children under five attending primary schools on a part-time basis is increasing although it remains only a small proportion of the total – seven per cent in 1988. The number of children within special schools remains constant. Under fives within independent schools are insignificant as a proportion of the total within local education authority provision, but are increasing.

Table 2.3: Education services for under fives UK, 1985 and 1988

	1985 No. of places (full- and part-time)	Places as % of population aged 3-4	1988 No. of places (full- and part-time)	Places as % of population aged 3-4
LEA nursery schools and classes	338,541	23	359,310	25
LEA primary schools	295,202	20	297,082	20
LEA special schools	6,000	0.4	6,000	0.4
Independent schools	35,000	2.4	40,000	2.7

Source: Cohen (1990)

Play and family support services

Playgroups

Provide play and learning opportunities for three and four year olds, and support through self-help for parents. In general attended two or three times a week and usually open for two or three hours 40 weeks of the year. Principal providers are voluntary self-help groups and private individuals or groups. Around three per cent are run by local authorities. Usually some charge for parents.

Parent and toddler groups

Provide opportunities for parents with young children to meet for a few hours once or twice a week. Provided by voluntary self-help groups or agencies and sometimes by local authorities. Usually small charge to cover refreshments or room hire.

Playbuses

Provide range of services including playgroups and parent and toddler groups on mobile basis to rural areas or groups such as travellers' children, badly served by other provision. Usually meet no more than once or twice a week for two or three hours. Run by voluntary groups and local authorities. In general a small charge.

Drop-in centres

Offer parents opportunity to 'drop in' with their children on regular or irregular basis to meet with others. In general open for a few hours a day, once or twice a week. Principal providers local authority and voluntary community workers and voluntary groups. Usually free with occasional charge for refreshments.

Family centres

Provide a wide range of services, both client-based, such as counselling or therapy for families with difficulties, or broader community services (sometimes combined with education) such as daycare, play and holiday schemes and adult educational and leisure activities. Principal providers: local authorities and voluntary agencies. Charges usually low and earning related.

Creches

Provide care for children in a group for short periods of time while parents are on the premises but involved in other activities such as conferences, classes, training, shopping and meetings. May be wide range of providers including educational and training organisations, voluntary groups, shopping centres, etc. Education and training provision usually free or low cost. Other provision variable.

Who gets play and family support

There were 490,515 playgroup places accounting for 34 per cent of three and four year olds in 1988 (Cohen, 1990) increasing from 32 per cent in 1985. As a proportion of the places are used in 'shifts' they are used by more children, probably around half of all three and four year olds. However, the overwhelming majority of playgroups are only open for up to four or five half-day sessions per week and the average attendance is only five hours per week. In many areas, playgroups have started to come under pressure from other services, in particular, nursery education and services providing daycare. A slow decrease in the number of playgroups has been predicted for the 1990s. (Statham)

No national statistics are available for parent and toddler groups, and drop in centres where the parent is in attendance. Family centres are, in general, not distinguished from local authority day nurseries. Northern Ireland has 27 statutory and voluntary family centres. It is not known what proportion of local authority and voluntary day nurseries elsewhere are family centres.

Care depends on where you live

Table 2.4: Selected local authority provision, 1988. Rates per 1000 children under five

	Local authority day nursery places	Private and voluntary day nursery places	Registered child minder places	LEA nursery education	Registered playgroup places
Camden	63	63	64	88	76
Brent	48	50	127	123	67
Tower Hamlets	31	9	28	176	37
Kensington	49	164	36	77	65
Herts	2	3	36	121	98
Manchester	39	12	32	219	52
North Tyneside	8	2	52	206	55
Gloucestershire	1	21	102	0	190
Wolverhampton	15	1	14	231	78
West Sussex	0	12	57	14	226
Lancashire	17	15	58	68	119
Cornwall	0	2	29	55	206

Source: Department of Health (1989,b); DES, 1989; Thomas Coram Research Unit.

Services are distributed unevenly both between different regions within the UK and within regions and districts (see table 2.4). There is, for example, significantly more day nursery provision in England and Scotland as in Northern Ireland and Wales and well over twice the proportion of Scottish three and four year olds are in nursery education as in Northern Ireland. There are few day nurseries in rural areas and a number of English rural authorities, including Devon, Cornwall and Sussex, the Scottish island authorities of Orkney and Shetland and half of the Welsh authorities had no local authority day nursery provision at all in 1988. Within London, parents of under fives in Tower Hamlets, for example, have far less access to daycare but greater access to nursery education than many other London boroughs. In some rural authorities, playgroups are the only extensive form of provision despite rising levels of demand in many rural areas. (SCAFA)

The continuity gap

A lack of continuity in a child's day or week occurs if parents have to use several services and arrangements to meet their own care requirements or simply because the hours available in one service do not meet the child's needs. The co-existence of overlapping services in some areas, with some services rationed, can involve children moving through several services within a short space of time. This is particularly evident in the immediate pre-school period where children may move from playgroups to nursery education into the reception class within the space of two years. There is also evidence of children attending more than one playgroup or using a playgroup in the morning and a nursery class in the afternoon. (Statham et al)

School age childcare services

Extended school hours schemes

Provide care and play and/or educational opportunities outside school hours on school premises. Usual hours from 8.30am - 6pm, 48-50 weeks of the year. Provided by local authorities. In general free.

School-based centres

Provide care and play and/or educational opportunities. Hours are variable, full provision 7.30 or 8am - 6pm. The principal providers are voluntary and community groups and local authorities. Variable cost.

Community-based centres

Provide care (including transport to centre) and play and/or educational activities in centres outside the school. As with school-based centres, hours are variable. Principal providers are voluntary and community groups and local authorities. Variable cost.

Childminders and nannies

Provide care outside school hours. In general, parents pay full cost.

School or community-based services are few in number with slightly more community-based schemes. A government Circular issued in 1989 seeks to extend the school-based form of provision through encouraging education authorities and school governing bodies to offer their premises for such schemes. The Circular stipulates that use would normally be self-financing or assisted by employers, a stipulation that most regard as unrealistic. There are also a wide variety of play and recreational schemes run by local authorities, community groups and others and used extensively by children and young people which do not have an explicit care element.

Who gets school age childcare

There are no nationally available statistics on school age childcare schemes. A 1989 survey carried out by Kids Clubs Network found only 320 schemes in the whole of the UK, providing places for less than 0.2 per cent of primary school children. A small proportion of provision is publicly provided. There are no nationally available statistics on childminders and nannies providing school age childcare. A 1980 survey found that 15 per cent of the arrangements made by working mothers for school aged children involved a childminder or friend, and three per cent nannies and au pairs. (Martin and Roberts)

Work and family employment provision

Both the demand and the nature of requirement for childcare services may be to some extent determined by working hours, the availability of work and employment provision.

Hours of work

A majority (66 per cent) of women with a child under five who are in paid employment work less than 30 hours per week. The majority of fathers with a child in this age group work 40 or more hours per week; UK fathers work the longest hours in Europe. As shown in Table 2.5 and 2.6, the working hours of mothers and fathers with a child under 10 are increasing. Fifteen per cent of mothers of under fives and 13 per cent of mothers of children aged five to nine are now working 40 or more hours per week compared with 11 per cent for both groups in 1985.

Table 2.5: Hours worked per week by employed mothers with child aged 0-9, 1985 and 1988 (percentages)

Hours normally	Child aged 0-4		Child aged 5-9	
worked per week	1985	1988	1985	1988
less than 20	51.0	44.8	49.2	45.2
20-29	18.1	20.8	22.3	24.1
30-39	19.6	19.2	16.6	17.0
40-49	8.4	11.1	8.1	9.1
50	2.6	3.4	3.2	4.3
Variable not determined	0.3	0.7	0.6	0.3

Source: Cohen, 1990

Table 2.6: Hours worked per week by employed fathers with child aged 0-9, 1985 and 1988 (percentages)

Hours normally	Child aged 0-4		Child aged 5-9	
worked per week	1985	1988	1985	1988
Less than 20	0.6	0.7	0.5	0.6
20-29	0.7	1.0	0.6	0.9
30-39	20.6	17.4	19.8	17.1
40-49	48.0	45.9	47.1	43.8
50 or more	29.6	34.5	31.3	37.1
Variable not determined	0.5	0.5	0.7	0.5

Source: Cohen, 1990

Maternity provision

An ILO Convention of 1911 recommended that the right to return to work following childbirth should be available to all employed pregnant women. However, the only maternity entitlement available to all employed pregnant women in the UK is that of paid time off for antenatal care. The other entitlements are only available subject to hours and service requirements. Recent survey evidence found that 40 per cent of employed pregnant women failed to qualify for the right to return to work following childbirth, rising to over half of semi-skilled and unskilled manual workers. (McRae and Daniel)

Where women do qualify, the relative brevity of the period for which adequate payment is made influences the time they return to work. Early survey evidence found that the median time of return was 15 weeks (Daniel) and that for women who do not qualify for statutory entitlement the return to work was 11 weeks.

Some of the demand for provision for childcare for very young babies arises from the lack of entitlement to maternity provision. Contractual provision does not substantially improve this situation. A 1989 survey found that only one in five employers had agreements which improved the basic minimum statutory provisions (Industrial Relations Review and Report, 1989b), and much of this provision in the public sector.

Preliminary findings of the Policy Studies Institute survey of maternity provision carried out on behalf of the Department of Employment, Department of Social Security and the Equal Opportunities Commission found little increase in arrangements by employers, particularly in the private sector, to help working parents.

Paternity, parental and family leave

There is no statutory entitlement in the UK to any of these forms of leave - now becoming increasingly common within Europe. Paternity leave is leave for fathers at or around the birth of their child. Parental or childcare leave allows mothers and fathers (but not at the same time) a period of paid leave after the end of maternity leave to provide and care themselves for their child. Family leave is leave related to children (sickness, for example or medical visits) or the care of the elderly or disabled dependants. The lack of these forms of leave means that fathers have no access to any statutory leave relating to the birth and care of their children. It influences the extent and nature of demand for childcare services and women's hours of work. Lack of family leave can contribute to the inability of women to take up full time employment – part-time work allows them to 'switch' days when children are ill.

It has been the government's policy for some time to encourage employers to offer these forms of provision but it has opposed the European Commission's parental leave proposals, believing parental leave should be offered by employers but not on a statutory basis. However, contractual provision in these areas ranges from limited to virtually non-existent.

Flexible working hours

The part-time work which characterises the employment of women with a child under 10 may reflect the absence of childcare services or preference for spending more time with the child. In the UK there is no statutory entitlement as in some countries to a reduction in working hours. However, in certain circumstances, women have successfully been able to claim indirect sex discrimination if an employer has refused to allow a woman to alter or reduce her hours following her return to work after childbirth. This has encouraged some employers to agree a return to part-time work following childbirth. Only women can gain access to flexible hours in this way.

Table 2.7: Work and family employment entitlements

Provision	Statutory	Contractual
Maternity leave	Right to stop work from 11 weeks prior to birth and return up to 29 weeks after, subject to 2 year service requirement for employees working 16 or more hours a week, 5 years for those working between 8 and 16 hours.	Limited improvement including service requirements and extended leave. More common in public sector.
Maternity pay	6 weeks at 90 per cent of earnings (subject to same hours and service requirements as to the right to return), 12 weeks low flat rate payment (subject to 26 weeks service requirement)	Limited improvement
Paternity leave	No statutory entitlement	IRRR survey* found 30 per cent of organisations provided paternity leave, most commonly 2 days
Parental leave	No statutory entitlement	Extremely rare
Adoptive parents	No statutory entitlement	IRRR survey* – offered by 10 per cent of organisations
Family leave	No statutory entitlement	Very limited provision
Career breaks	No statutory entitlement	IRRR survey* – 5 per cent of organisations
Reduced working	No statutory entitlement	IRRR survey* – 30 per cent of organisations allowed women to work part time on return to work

*Industrial Relations Review and Report 439 and 442 based on random sample of employers subscribing to IRRR and therefore in most cases offering better employment provisions than teneral.

Shortfall in provision

Between 1985 and 1988, when demand was rising significantly, the number of places in local authority nurseries increased by only four per cent and in nursery education by only six per cent. In the same period, publicly funded services in both Denmark and France (already at a much higher level than in the UK) increased by 14 per cent.

In the UK, access to publicly-funded services is limited to two per cent of children under three, and between 35 and 40 per cent of three and four year olds. Fewer than 0.5 per cent of primary school children have access to care out of school hours. Among three and four year olds, only 25 per cent are in nursery education, and this is generally part-time. A further 20 per cent are in primary schools, where staffing levels and the teaching curriculum are not geared to the needs of this age group. Playgroups are providing many more children with valuable opportunities for learning through play, but the average attendance is only five hours per week. All this offers UK children a much more limited experience than they would get elsewhere in Europe: in France, for example, more than 95 per cent of three and four year olds are in nursery education, generally full-time.

UK services also fail to meet the cultural and linguistic requirements of particular ethnic groups and communities. Childcare can play an important part in protecting cultural and linguistic identities, but this is seldom acknowledged.

The shortfall resulting from current levels of provision has a qualitative as well as a quantitative dimension. (See p.31 for social and economic impact.) Services or employment entitlements which are currently available are not necessarily those which most effectively meet the needs of, or are preferred by, parents and children. The absence of recent survey data or of meaningful waiting lists for many forms of provision makes assessing potential consumer demand difficult.

Under fives shortfall

The most recent national survey of demand for services was carried out as long ago as 1974 (see table 2.8). This found that some form of day provision was wanted by mothers for twice as many children as were then using it. While 32 per cent of children were using facilities, 64 per cent wanted them, with the demand greatest for older pre-school children: provision was wanted for 90 per cent of four year olds and 20 per cent of those aged under one. The gap between supply and demand was greatest for two year olds - with only eight per cent using provision, while 41 per cent required it.

The survey also found a significant 'consumer' gap: a great majority of mothers whose children were with childminders wanted other forms of provision with a strong preference for educational provision.

Table 2.8: Use of services compared with expressed preferences

	Service used	Service preferred
Nursery school/class	9%	20%
Day nursery	2%	7%
Childminder	3%	3%
Playgroup	18%	25%
Creche	1%	1%
More than one type	Not available	1%
Already in primary school (included with nursery school)		3%
None	68%	37%
Not known		2%

Source: Bone

Table 2.9: Parental preference and use (in brackets) according to child's age (percentages)

Type of day provision preferred	All ages	Up to 1 year	1 year	2 years	3 years	4 years
Educational services (nursery/primary)	20 (9)	1 (–)	4 (–)	16 (1)	35 (9)	41 (33)
Day nurseries	7 (2)	6 (–)	9 (1)	9 (2)	8 (3)	5 (3)
Childminders	3 (3)	6 (2)	4 (3)	3 (3)	1 (3)	2 (3)
Playgroups	25 (18)	4 (1)	19 (3)	39 (13)	37 (34)	21 (35)

Source: Bone

The consumer gap

The rise in maternal employment rates has contributed to a strengthening in demand since 1974. A 1988 survey of 1,000 families in Strathclyde (Scott) found a widening gap between parents wanting and using daycare, with day nurseries preferred by more than four times as many as using them. However, it also shows a continuing strong preference for nursery education relative to its actual use. The use of playgroups significantly exceeded stated preference for three and four year olds.

What can we conclude from this? Preference surveys always have to be treated with some caution. In addition, it should be noted that the preference surveys shown here do not include nannies or a paid leave option. A parental leave option would itself reduce the shortfall in services for children under one and to a lesser extent under two years of age considerably. Taking account of employment rates and expressed employment intentions as well as expressed preferences for particular forms of provision, it is evident that the shortfall in services is considerable.

The 1974 Bone survey shows that even then there was a considerable shortfall in the provision of daycare in particular for under threes with day nurseries wanted by six per cent of mothers with a child under one and nine per cent of one and two year olds. Childminders were required for under twos by more mothers than were using them, and there was no information on nannies. Since the Bone survey, rates of employment for mothers of under fives has increased from 26 per cent to 37 per cent, and there is now strong evidence that the majority of economically inactive women with a child under five would wish to enter employment or education if affordable childcare were available. The Strathclyde survey of 1,000 families found that under a quarter of economically inactive women with a child under five would want to stay at home if childcare was available and affordable. Daycare places are only available for around eight per cent of under fives.

Bone showed a shortfall in less formal provision of playgroups for children under three – this seems to have been substantially filled by parent and toddlers' groups and the Strathclyde survey shows that the use of playgroups for three and four year olds significantly exceeds preference. For children over three there is a strong parental preference for nursery education which current levels of provision are not meeting.

The increase in maternal employment, as well as women's expressed intentions of going out to work if suitable child care were available, suggests that while parents want nursery education they are likely also to want care. There are currently publicly funded places (full and part-time) for 19 per cent of UK under fives in local authority day nursery and educational provision. Our cost benefit analyis (see Part Two) is based on models which provide places in publicly-funded childcare for between 34 and 58 per cent of under fives.

School age shortfall

Demand for school age childcare and preference between different forms of provision has been relatively unexplored. Employment rates of mothers of school age children have been substantially higher than for pre-school children although the gap is now narrowing and the shortfall has been assessed in relation to the inadequacies of arrangements rather than expressed demand. Some of this information has been derived from estimates of children left unattended. A 1978 report estimated that 300,000 of five to 10 year olds and 375,000 of 11-15 year olds were left unsupervised during the school holidays, while 225,000 of five to 10 year olds and 300,000 of 11-15 year olds were left unattended after school. (Simpson)

A survey carried out in London in 1985 indicates the extent to which mothers of school age children are affected in their employment by the lack of childcare and are frequently forced to give up employment because of childcare problems. Over half of mothers of seven to 11 year olds who are not in paid employment had left jobs because of childcare problems. (Petrie and Logan)

There are currently publicly funded places for less than 0.2 per cent of primary school children. Our cost-benefit analysis (see Part Two) is based on models which provide places for between 15 per cent and 53 per cent of five to 11 year olds.

Employment provisions shortfall

As we have seen, many UK mothers have no right to maternity leave. Nor do UK parents have access to parental leave – that is, time off work, following the expiry of maternity leave (which covers the post-natal period) to look after very small children. Nor do they enjoy a range of entitlements for working parents which have been developed in the European Community over the past decade. Overall, the UK is one of the poorest providers in the European Community, comparing particularly badly with Denmark, France and Belgium.

Lack of adequate employment provisions, including adequate paid maternity leave, paternity and parental leave, must be considered as part of the shortfall in provision.

Consumers deprived of choice

'Diversity' in provision has been presented as a strength of the current structure of provision. In the 1989 debate on the Education Select Committee Report on educational provisions for under fives, the Secretary of State for Education welcomed the diversity of provision which the Select Committee itself supported.

> The Government are . . . committed to the continuation of a range of provisions that will meet a variety of needs in both the public and private sectors. (Statham et al)

However, the substantial shortfall in provision combined with geographical inequity, income differentials and other restrictions on access effectively deprive consumers of choice. Parents play a very large role as funders and unpaid volunteers, but only a minor role as consumers in determining the nature and availability of both services and employment provision.

SOCIAL AND ECONOMIC IMPACT

The structure and low levels of childcare services, and the absence or inadequacy of relevant employment provisions, have a significant social and economic impact. Inadequacies in provision create inequity in opportunities for both children and women, affect the participation of men within family life, contribute to high levels of family poverty and reflect and contribute to regional and community disadvantage.

Social impact

On children

Children require services for a variety of reasons. Sometimes (and increasingly) this is because their parents are in paid employment or education; sometimes (and again increasingly) because, with smaller families and a 'child unfriendly' environment, it is the only way they can meet and play safely with other children. Sometimes it is because of the inadequacy of family care and, for all children, because of the opportunities which high quality services can provide in assisting their educational and social development.

The low level and uneven distribution of services combined with an uneven and fragmented structure and the existence of financial and other constraints on access to services produces considerable inequity in children's pre-school experience and the levels of public support they receive.

Some children have access to nursery education - fully publicly funded - many more do not. For children whose parents are in paid employment or education, the availability of services and level of parental income determines the form and often the quality of the care they receive. As already noted, most children in this situation are cared for through informal arrangements. Sometimes, this is through parental choice; most often, through the lack of any alternative.

Of formal services, the one most extensively used - childminding - receives very little or no public support and is not the preferred option of many parents. For children whose parents are not in paid employment, even part-time daycare is only an option for the better off or for those categorised as 'in need' for whom too often it is provided in an apartheid form separating them from other children.

Lacking access to the kind of community-based provision (accessible and affordable to all families), which has developed or is developing in countries such as France, Italy and Scandinavia, UK children thus find their access to childcare frequently determined by their parents' employment or income status or by the stigma of 'need'.

The private sector is becoming increasingly important as a provider of day care. This, together with the inability of local authorities to respond to growing daycare demand, is exacerbating inequity within provision. Available evidence suggests that developments in day nursery provision are favouring more advantaged groups and communities. In London, for example, which has a declining proportion of children in publicly funded provision, Kensington had day nursery provision in 1988 for 21 per cent of under fives, Wandsworth 12 per cent and Islington 10 per cent, compared with Tower Hamlets, which had places for only four per cent of under fives. A recent survey of more than 70 day nurseries in four local authorities found that newly registered private nurseries were providing almost exclusively for professional and high income groups. (Penn)

For school age children, the lack of out of school provision means that 'self-care' is often the only option. It is estimated that around 30 per cent of primary school children are 'latchkey kids'. The costs of not providing services outside school hours are accidents, vandalism and crime.

Access to quality in services

Recent examination of international research has emphasised the importance of the quality of daycare as a mediating factor in relation to child development. (Schaffer; Melhuish and Moss). The quality of the service is not necessarily synonymous with its cost but a number of factors associated with quality do have significant cost and funding implications. Broadly these relate, in nursery provision, to the training, pay and conditions of childcare workers and, more specifically to the staff-child ratio all of which can determine the quality of the staff-child relationship. A recent US study of daycare centres has shown that the most important predictor of the quality of care is staff wages, with low wages contributing directly to high staff turnover. (National Child Care Staffing Study)

In the UK, there has been only a limited examination of the quality of daycare services but it is known that the pay and conditions of many groups of childcare workers are generally inadequate. In 1985, for example, the only workers in the pre-school services earning more than half the average non-manual male wage were teachers in nursery education. Childminders were earning less than a quarter of the average non-manual male wage, a factor contributing to a very high turnover among childminders. (Cohen, 1988)

Private sector childcare workers, in particular, have poor pay and conditions of employment. A 1980 study of the private and public sector nurseries found that private sector nurseries had staff with lower levels of training and qualifications and a lower staff-child ratio. The Penn 1990 survey found the private nurseries to be of variable quality with generally poor premises, limited curriculum, limited mention of gender issues and no attention paid to race or disability, but notes a small number of 'outstanding' nurseries, including some company nurseries and one (with the highest fees) providing almost exclusively for high-income professionals. The Penn survey found that 60 per cent of all the nurseries experienced problems of staff turnover and that wages in general were low, starting at £2.50 to £3.50 per hour with only senior staff earning more than £100 per week. (Garland and White; Penn).

In so far as quality is cost related, children from low income families are not only disadvantaged in terms of access to formal provision, but may be doubly disadvantaged in terms of their access to quality provision. The introduction of the 1989 Children Act reflected recognition of the need to improve the quality of services, but the available evidence suggests that public funding as well as public regulation is required if services are to be delivered on an equitable basis.

The 1989 Children Act makes local authorities responsible for providing daycare for children in need. But daycare is defined as any form of care or supervised activity during the day whether or not it is provided on a regular basis. In addition, needs-based provision, frequently catering only for children or families with identified problems, not only sets up its own 'service trap' similar in its effect to the benefit trap but leads to stigmatisation of the services themselves. This makes some parents who might qualify reluctant to use them.

Childcare at home

While the lack of interest in developing daycare services in the UK may be partly attributed to the persisting view that mothers should stay at home and care for their children themselves, parental care options in the home are being left to accident rather than design. As with services, it is an option that is more readily available as a considered choice for advantaged rather than disadvantaged groups. In the absence of adequate statutory provision, some women may have to return to work within a few weeks; while the virtual absence of parental leave deprives babies from being cared for by their fathers.

Little is known about the quality of care provided for children in their own home in their parents' absence, but the lack of regulation of nannies and babysitters and the use of friends and relatives can be less than ideal. A recent study of Italian toddlers examined the care and activities of children aged between 12 and 36 months not attending day nurseries. Of these, 57 per cent were being cared for by mothers, 25 per cent by grandmothers and 17 per cent by babysitters and others. Between the hours of 6am and 10pm, 27 per cent spent nine of the 16 hours with only one adult, 36 per cent spent more than 13 hours without meeting a child (if siblings were excluded this proportion rose to 80 per cent). Over a half never played outside, and 36 per cent watched television. (Musatti)

For UK children under three, parent and toddler and drop-in services provide both parents and children with opportunities for social interaction and support, but do not offer the more organised flexible care options which are, for example, provided in France through the extended *halte garderie* (short-term care centres). Local survey evidence in the UK suggests many parents would like this form of care irrespective of whether they are in paid employment or education. (SCAFA)

Less care, more poverty

The failure to provide either for parental care through employment entitlements such as paid parental leave or for daycare services facilitating parent employment has contributed directly to the high levels of child poverty in this country. A 1990 Child Poverty Action Group report identifies 3,090,000 children as living in households with below 50 per cent of average income - a commonly used poverty measure (Oppenheim). We estimate that just under a third of under fives - a higher proportion than of all children - are living in households with below 50 per cent of average income. This amounts to one and a quarter million under fives.

Numbers living in households with less than 50 per cent of national average income is a commonly accepted measure of poverty throughout the European Community; the incidence of children below this national 'poverty line' in the UK is the third highest in the EC. When the 'poverty line' is drawn at 50 per cent of the EC average income, the UK has the fifth highest incidence of child poverty. (CEC, 1991)

An analysis of Department of Social Security data has shown that children living in poverty are more likely to be living in a household where the mother does not work. In 1981 over half of families where both parents were working were in the top two income quintiles and only three per cent in the bottom quintile. Where only the husband was working, over four times as many (13 per cent) were in the bottom quintile.

Inadequacies in general provision for all parents become acute for lone parents and have unacceptable consequences for children themselves. Child poverty is particularly associated with single parenthood. One-parent families are more likely than other families to be in the bottom quintile, even when the parent is employed. However, only 15 per cent of the families of employed lone parents were in the bottom quintile in 1981 compared with 66 per cent of those where the parent was not employed. (Brown; Moss, 1989)

In Australia, a widely accepted political objective that no child should live in poverty has brought an examination of the role of childcare services in helping families out of poverty. A cost benefit study commissioned by the Australian Government has pointed to the role of public childcare in reducing inequalities in the distribution of family incomes and in offering longterm protection against poverty arising from separation, divorce or widowhood. (Cass)

Children as citizens

The UN Convention on the Rights of the Child, which the UK is expected to ratify shortly (with, it is thought, significant reservations) has illuminated the issue of child citizenship. While the UN Convention seeks to protect and empower children in contradistinction to the rights of parents and others, it also recognises the mutuality of interest between child and parents. Article 18.3 requires that states 'shall take all appropriate measures to ensure that children of working parents have the right to benefit from childcare services and facilities for which they are eligible'. Articles 26 and 27, which specify the right for children to benefit from social security and to enjoy an adequate standard of living, have focussed attention on the role of daycare (as described above) in bringing children out of poverty, and the current inadequacy of what has been described as the UK child's 'badge of citizenship' - child benefit. (Lister)

The wider debate on child citizenship engendered by the Convention raises similar questions over inequity in access to services which provide opportunities for learning and development, and the importance of a structure of services which fully meets the needs of all children. If high quality pre-school services have a lasting benefit throughout childhood and in assisting in the transition to responsible adult citizenship - as the evidence suggests - then it is important that all children have access to such services, with additional consideration paid to the particular needs of some groups (see below).

Children with special needs. UK legislation has recognised the value of integrated provision as an important precursor to the integrated adult citizenship of children with special needs. However, the under-resourcing of special help for such children has made this difficult to achieve. An integrated setting may, for many of these children, be at the expense of additional help and respite, and the number of children under five in special schools remained constant between 1985 and 1988. (Cohen, 1990.

Children from black and ethnic minority groups. Black and minority ethnic groups experience disproportionate disadvantages, such as bad housing and educational underachievement. This may increase their need of provision: West Indian/Guyanese and Indian women with pre-school children have higher rates of employment than other women and therefore a greater need of daycare. Problems of access are frequently compounded for these groups by institutional and individual racism. Recognition of the rights of these children as citizens involves recognition of their language and cultural and social values to ensure the availability of provision to meet these needs.

The privatisation of daycare has particular implications for these groups. Evidence suggests that parents from black and minority ethnic groups are likely to experience greater difficulty in finding and keeping a place with a childminder, and that Afro-Caribbean mothers are more likely to end up with poor quality childminders. (Mayall and Petrie)

Indigenous non-English speaking children. Pre-school provision has a recognised role in preserving language and its cultural associates. Inadequate access to services serving this function is a major issue for those parts of the UK where English is not or has not traditionally been the vernacular. Welsh and Gaelic medium provision is, in general, limited to playgroups rarely offering more than a few sessions a week thus making them (for some parents) difficult to use and diminishing their effectiveness in maintaining the use of the language.

Women

Women are affected by the lack of maternity provision, while the absence of paternity and parental leave reinforces the unequal sharing of childcare responsibilities within the family. It is women rather than men who are most affected by the availability and cost of services, with many women unable to continue in paid employment or education or being restricted in their hours of work and/or employment choices. Research evidence has shown that child-bearing and child-rearing substantially reduce employment experience and earnings potential, costing the average UK mother of two more than half of her potential lifetime's earnings. (Joshi, 1987)

Employment rates for women are increasing, and women are expected to fill 90 per cent of a projected overall increase of one million new jobs by the year 2000 (EOC, 1990). However, the pay gap between men and women has not narrowed significantly since the late 1970s, and in 1990 women's average gross hourly earnings were 77 per cent of that of men (EOC, 1991). The income differential is much wider because of the differences in hours of work (see tables 2.5 and 2.6, p.21).

The impact on lone mothers is much greater. Inadequate recognition of childcare costs within the income support system, together with the difficulties of meeting childcare needs, has contributed, as we have seen, to very low employment rates amongst UK lone mothers. Only 18 per cent of lone mothers with a child under five are in paid employment and only six per cent of these are in full-time employment - the lowest rate in the European community.

Men

Men's employment experience and earnings are largely unaffected by fatherhood. However, their experience as fathers is considerably affected by their employment role. Fathers have no access to statutory leave in relation to the birth or care of their children, and employee entitlements in this area are very limited (see p.24). In addition, the hours of work of many fathers are increasing. As noted, UK fathers of under fives have the longest working hours in Europe with more than a third working 50 hours a week or more. Lack of recognition given to the role of fathers in caring for children not only places additional stress on women but can make it more difficult for fathers to establish a close relationship with their children.

One study has reported the extent to which middle-class fathers feel themselves to be shadowy figures in the background of the family while fathers of younger children feel their children scarcely recognise them. Another study which looked at the relation of fathers to child-birth and work found many fathers wanting time off work around the time of childbirth, not only to help the mother practically and emotionally but also to establish their own relationship with the child (Elliott; Bell et el). There is growing evidence that a close relationship with both parents benefits children: with no supportive provision, fathers have considerable difficulties achieving this.

In Sweden, a range of employment provisions accessible to fathers in relation to the birth and care of their children is leading to an increase in fathers' participation in childcare. In 1987, 41 per cent of parents taking leave to care for a sick child were fathers, as were 34 per cent of those taking leave to visit their child's nursery or school. (EC Childcare Network, b).

The economic impact

The economic impact of inadequate childcare provision has received far less recognition than its social impact but its significance is increasingly recognised and has now led to some funding from the European Commission's Structural Funds (see p.54).

Impact on the labour market

Low levels of provision affect both the levels and nature of women's participation on the labour market.

Quantitative impact

Inadequate childcare provision imposes restrictions on the supply of labour contributing to the underlying inflationary pressures on the UK economy. While maternal employment rates have been increasing, they remain substantially lower than that for men and other women, and the overwhelming majority of economically active mothers with a child under the age of 10 continues to work part-time (45 per cent of them less than 20 hours a week). Full-time employment rates remain among the lowest in the European Community (see tables 4.4 to 4.6).

This serious under-utilisation of labour has disturbing implications in the context of demographic trends and the projected reduction in new entrants to the labour force. One study of nine out of the 12 members of the European Community projects that a net surplus in entrance into the European labour market of just under one million in 1981 will have become, by the year 2000, a net loss of 300,000.

Local surveys consistently show that a lack of suitable, affordable childcare is often one of the most important barriers to enhancing the supply of labour. A skills audit carried out for the city of Norwich found that lack of childcare facilities was the most significant impediment to employment within the area. (C.A.G. Consultants)

This author estimated for the Scottish Development Agency that the provision of suitable, affordable childcare could offset by approximately two-thirds the projected reduction in the Glasgow labour market. (Scottish Development Agency).

These general constraints on the supply of labour are experienced by employers both in terms of recruitment and by unnecessarily low rates of return to employment of women following childbirth. While the proportion of women back in work within nine months of childbirth has increased - from a quarter in 1979 to nearly a half in 1988, rates of return to existing employment are lower, and significantly so in the private sector (McRae and Daniel). An annual loss of around 700 members of staff per annum - with significant implications in terms of recruitment and training costs - prompted the Midland Bank to embark on developing a nursery programme with plans for opening 200 nurseries for its employees. However, only a tiny minority of employers are sufficiently aware of the loss or have the resources to take such action.

Qualitative impact

Inadequacies in childcare provision also affect the quality of labour supply in a number of ways:

Low uptake in education and training. The effects of the lack of childcare provision on women's participation in further and higher education can be inferred from the drop in the proportion of women students aged 20-30 (the prime childbearing years). Survey evidence also shows that a significant proportion of currently economically inactive women would undertake further education or training if childcare were available (Scott; SCAFA). This is of particular significance in areas requiring economic regeneration.

A gender segregated labour market. Women are heavily concentrated in relatively few occupations, frequently those with a large pool of part-time labour. In 1987, women constituted only nine per cent of those in professional and related (science, engineering technology) fields, but 75 per cent of those in catering, cleaning, hairdressing and other personal services, and 74 per cent of clerical and related jobs. This segregation reflects both the constraints upon women's access to employment and the stereotyping within education and employment – the expectation made by girls and women that some areas are 'not for them'. Good equal opportunity practice (relating to sex, race and disability) within high quality childcare services can reduce stereotype expectations and thus have an impact on labour recruitment.

Skill shortages. Under-utilisation of women combined with job segregation and stereotyping contributes to the problem of skill shortages - again adding to inflationary pressures. Surveys show a significant skill loss represented by economically inactive women with children. A study in Ross and Cromarty of women returners to the labour market found that of those women not currently in work, 11 per cent were educated to degree level, 18 per cent had diplomas above the level of highers (for example, a diploma of college education or as a state registered nurse) and 44 per cent had qualifications of one higher or above (Mann; SCAFA).

This and previously cited surveys showing significant demand for education and training among currently economically inactive women with children underlines the role which childcare can play in enhancing skill levels, particularly within more disadvantaged communities.

Impact on children as they grow to adulthood

Pre-school provision also has long-term benefits for communities. Studies have identified that the benefits of pre-school programmes in the development and educational potential of children are long-lasting and extensive. (Weikart; Osborne and Milbank). No study has been made of the effect on children's development of satisfactory out of school hours provision. The findings of the US Ypsilanti study (see below) of the effects of early education on disadvantaged children has been influential in the New Zealand government's work on childcare reforms.

The Ypsilanti study

Educational achievement: Children with pre-school experience are more likely to complete schooling than those who do not, and spend fewer years in remedial classes. Thirty-eight per cent went on to post-secondary education.

Employment: Children with pre-school experience are more likely to be employed as young adults, and are more likely to support themselves completely on their own savings.

Delinquency: Children with pre-school experience are less likely to be arrested by the age of 19 than those with no pre-school experience.

Teenage pregnancy: Girls with pre-school experience are less likely to be teenage mothers and more likely to have jobs.

Paying for itself: Savings in cost of remedial education, unemployment benefit and prison was estimated at $400-$700 for each $100 spent. (Weikart) The benefits of daycare are likely to be greatest for children for whom the quality of home care is poor. For very young infants with high-quality home care, the benefits of daycare will necessarily be less or even non-existent.

Quality care requires resourcing both in terms of services and in ensuring quality home care through paid parental leave. Public contributions to educational achievement, redressing the effects of economic and social disadvantage, and contributing to the healthy development of children have wider economic as well as social benefits for the community as a whole.

Role of childcare in economic regeneration

While the factors outlined above are relevant to all parts of the country, they can have an enhanced significance in some disadvantaged areas - both rural and urban. This has a number of dimensions.

In Scotland, the role of childcare in strategies for economic regeneration in disadvantaged areas has been recognised by the Scottish Development Agency (now Scottish Enterprise) and an increasing number of local authorities. One interesting example of its potential role in rural development is that of a project currently being established by a group of women in South Uist in the Western Isles in which childcare is seen as crucial - enhancing the educational opportunities of the children, and giving women access to training and employment and so assisting in the diversification of the local economy. It also offers earlier and more regular access to Gaelic, and thus strengthens the linguistic identity and hence confidence of the community in its own future.

CHILDCARE IN EUROPE

Changes affecting families and their social provision needs are taking place throughout the European Community. All member states have experienced substantial (and continuing) growth in the demand for services. Reports prepared for the European Commission by the Commission's Childcare Network, established in 1986, found inadequate provision throughout the Community and concern in all member states about the quality of both services and employment entitlements.

Key issues identified by the Childcare Network

- The level and quality of services for children under three and childcare services for school age children
- the low level of services in many rural areas where maternal employment is increasing and so is demand
- the inadequate consideration of the needs of particular ethnic and linguistic groups
- the distinction between care and education services in many countries
- the poor pay and conditions of childcare workers, the majority of whom are women
- the unequal sharing of the care of children between women and men
- the need for employment provisions and other measures to assist employees in balancing their work and family commitments

Who provides what

The Network's reports have also revealed considerable variation in the level of services and policies between member states. Significantly, levels of provision in the United Kingdom are substantially poorer than in most other EC countries (see Table 4.1).

Table 4.1: EC publicly funded childcare services as a percentage of all children in age group

	Children under 3	Children from 3 to compulsory school age	Age when compulsory schooling begins
Belgium	20%	95%+	6 years
Denmark	48%	85%	7 years
France	20%	95%+	6 years
Germany	3%	65-70%	6-7 years
Greece	4%	65-70%	5.5 years
Ireland	2%	55%	6 years
Italy	5%	85%+	6 years
Luxembourg	2%	55-60%	5 years
Netherlands	2%	50-55%	5 years
Portugal	6%	35%	6 years
Spain		65-70%	6 years
United Kingdom*	2%	35-40%	5 years

Source: CEC, a

* Government statistics on European comparisons commonly include playgroups within UK provision for this age group. These are not included in the EC Childcare Network comparative tables as these are based on publicly funded places providing education or care for a significant period of time. Although a substantial minority of children attend playgroups in the UK, their average attendance is only 5 hours per week (compared with, for example, 30-40 hours per week in French nursery education), and only a third of playgroups receive any public funds, with an average grant covering less than 10 per cent of running costs. Informal provision of this kind such as drop-in centres and parent and toddler groups are excluded from these comparisons.

Table 4.1 shows the level of publicly funded services for children from 0 until they start school, which ranges from the age of four (in Northern Ireland) to seven in Denmark. Overall, the levels of services for children under three are low, although Belgium and France have places for 20 per cent of this age group, and Denmark has 48 per cent either in publicly run day nurseries or with employed childminders. This compares with two per cent of UK children under three within local authority day nurseries: many of these places are only available to children in need. For children from three to school age, levels of services are higher, with most countries providing two to three years of nursery education. In Belgium and France, nursery education is available, predominantly on a full-time basis, to over 95 per cent of three and four year olds. In France, nursery schools are open eight hours a day, from 8.30am to 4.30pm and most provide meals and supervision during the two-hour lunch break. (CEC, a)

In contrast, in the UK, only a quarter of three and four year olds are in nursery education and this is largely part-time (with only 15 per cent on a full-time or equivalent basis). In total, only 37 per cent of three to four year olds in the UK are in nursery education, primary schools, local authority day nurseries or using sponsored childminding places, the latter usually on welfare grounds.

School age childcare is a considerable problem in all member states. Only Denmark, where the school day itself is much shorter, has substantial provision providing for 29 per cent of primary school children. Portugal and Germany provide for 6 per cent and 4 per cent respectively, compared with less than 1 per cent in the United Kingdom. (CEC, a)

Employment Provisions

The UK is the only country in the European Community not to offer all employed pregnant women maternity leave (see Table 4.2). The only restrictions in all the other countries relate to fixed term contracts. In general, but not in the United Kingdom, the full period of leave is covered by earnings related payments.

Table 4.2: Maternity leave in EC member states

Belgium	14 weeks altogether; 8 weeks must be taken after birth, the other 6 weeks can be taken before or after. 75% of earnings (82% for first month)
Denmark	4 weeks before birth, 14 weeks after. 90% of earnings (up to a maximum level)
France	6 weeks before birth, 10 weeks after (longer for multiple births). 84% of earnings
Germany	6 weeks before birth, 8 weeks after (12 for multiple births). 100% of earnings
Greece	16 weeks, to be taken before or after birth. 100% of earnings
Ireland	14 weeks altogether; 4 weeks must be taken before birth, 4 weeks must be taken after and the other 6 weeks can be taken before or after. 70% of earnings (tax free). Mothers can request additional 4 weeks unpaid leave
Italy	2 months before birth, 3 months after. 80% of earnings
Luxembourg	6 weeks before birth, 8 weeks after (12 for multiple births). 100% of earnings
Netherlands	16 weeks altogether; 4-6 weeks can be taken before birth, 10-12 weeks after. 100% of earnings
Portugal	90 days altogether; 60 days must be taken after birth and the other 30 days can be taken before or after. 100% of earnings
Spain	16 weeks altogether; 10 weeks must be taken after birth and the other 6 weeks can be taken before or after. 75% of earnings
United Kingdom	11 weeks before birth, 29 weeks after. 90% of earnings for 6 weeks, low flat-rate payment for 12 weeks, no payment for remaining weeks. Eligibility depends on two years' service and number of hours worked per week.

Source: CEC, a

Parental leave

Parental or childcare leave is now available in seven countries for varying periods ranging from 10 weeks in Denmark to nearly three years in France. Some payment is made to some groups of parents in four of these countries, while in Denmark the payment is earnings related.

Table 4.3: Parental leave in EC member states

Belgium	None, but workers can take leave for family or personal reasons
Denmark	10 weeks. 90% of earnings (up to a maximum level)
France	Until child is 3. No payment unless 3 or more children; then low, flat-rate payment
Germany	18 months. Low flat-rate payment for 6 months; payment then depends on family income, so higher income family gets less
Greece	3 months per parent. Unpaid
Ireland	None.
Italy	6 months. 30% of earnings
Luxembourg	None
Netherlands	None, but government proposal for part-time leave has been made
Portugal	24 months. Unpaid
Spain	12 months. Unpaid
United Kingdom	None.

Source: CEC, a

Six countries also have statutory provision for parental leave to care for sick children. One country, Denmark, has paternity leave.

Parental employment

Employment rates for mothers have been increasing in all countries. the largest increases have been taking place in the Netherlands, the UK and Ireland.

Table 4.4: EC employment participation rates of mothers of children aged 0-4, 1988

Figures as percentage	Full time	Part time	Total in employment
Belgium	36.98	15.83	52.81
Denmark	45.86	28.89	74.75
France	37.51	14.23	51.74
***Germany**	15.63	18.08	33.70
Greece	33.01	6.49	39.50
Ireland	19.04	6.03	25.07
Italy	34.95	4.91	39.86
Luxembourg	27.09	9.20	36.29
Netherlands	4.17	24.77	28.94
Portugal	54.49	6.18	60.67
Spain	23.98	4.20	28.18
UK	11.26	25.27	36.53
Euro 12 (average)	24.79	15.13	39.92

*Federal Republic

Source: Cohen, 1990

Table 4.5: EC employment participation rates of mothers of children aged 5-9 , 1988

Figures as percentage	Full time	Part time	Total in employment
Belgium	35.71	16.09	51.80
Denmark	44.45	37.18	81.63
France	37.36	16.35	53.71
***Germany**	16.26	22.44	38.70
Greece	36.80	3.78	40.58
Ireland	12.28	7.35	19.63
Italy	36.53	4.81	41.34
Luxembourg	26.36	9.46	35.82
Netherlands	4.41	28.48	32.89
Portugal	54.94	6.24	61.18
Spain	22.20	4.39	26.59
UK	13.86	38.68	52.54
Euro 12 (average)	26.45	17.92	44.37

*Federal Republic

Source: Cohen, 1990

UK employment participation rates by mothers of dependent children continues to be characterised by a high proportion of part-time work. The full-time employment rate for mothers of under fives is the second lowest in the European Community, and for mothers of children aged five to nine the third lowest. As noted earlier, employment rates among lone mothers, unlike mothers in general, are scarcely increasing at all in the UK.

Table 4.6: EC employment participation rates of lone mothers of children aged 0-4, 1988

Figures as percentage	Full time	Part time	Total in employment
Belgium	32.09	10.04	42.13
Denmark	38.86	30.67	69.53
France	44.85	8.39	53.24
Germany	25.94	15.26	41.20
Greece	41.03	5.98	47.01
Ireland	13.13	3.85	16.98
Italy	52.90	4.72	57.62
Luxembourg	72.56	2.38	74.94
Netherlands	7.37	10.51	17.88
Portugal	55.96	9.23	65.19
Spain	43.89	5.86	49.75
UK	6.34	11.72	18.06
Euro 12 (average)	25.85	10.98	36.83

* Federal Republic

Source: Cohen, 1990

Policy development

Variations in levels of services reflect variations in policies, in particular to the access to services by working parents. The UK (together with Ireland) is unique in not acknowledging any public responsibility in the provision of daycare for working parents except where the children or families are 'in need'.

In Denmark, as early as 1964, legislation established that the provision of public daycare should not be seen as a residual function but as integral to the Danish welfare state, offering all children a place in public daycare (Moss, 1988). Acknowledgement of public responsibility in relation to daycare services has led to a wider programme including the development of employment provisions and the more general examination of work and family policies. Most recently, an inter-ministerial committee has been examining how to improve parents' working hours. (CEC, a)

A similar approach to daycare has been established in other countries. In Italy, legislation in 1971 recognised the right of working and non-working women to use nurseries (with priority to working mothers) and placed an obligation on the state to play an active role in setting up childcare services. In Belgium and France, funding arrangements have been changed to widen access to publicly provided and funded daycare. (Moss, 1988)

Recommendations of the European Commission's Childcare Network

The European Commission's Childcare Network concluded that inadequacies and disparities in both provision and policies were of concern for three reasons:

- they failed - to varying degrees - to meet the needs of families
- they undermined European equality legislation
- they constituted an obstacle to free movement of labour (of increasing significance as Europe moves towards integration). 'The current major disparities in childcare services and related policies affecting the employment of many workers with children are not compatible with the concept of a single European market.' (Moss, 1988)

The Network's principal recommendation was that states should be required through what is known as a 'framework' directive to develop publicly funded services. This requires member states to comply with the stated objectives without having to use specific models. Such a directive should, in the Network's view, require member states to ensure that services should be available for children at least up to the age of 10, with an ultimate objective of ensuring publicly funded services for all parents employed or training 'either free at the time of use or at a reasonable price that all parents can afford taking into account their income and other needs' (Moss,1988). Such a directive should be implemented by a guide to good practice in childcare services.

Other Network recommendations include directives relating to maternity, parental and family leave and a European programme to examine issues and problems concerning childcare and the reconciliation of parenthood and employment. Suggested minimum targets for expansion over a five-year period were for publicly funded full-time places for five to ten per cent of children under three, 60-70 per cent of children from three to compulsory school age and full-day childcare services for 10-15 per cent of children from three to ten. (Moss, 1988)

The Network's recommendation of a directive was supported by the Women's Committee of the European Parliament, which in a subsequent report expressed concern that without a legally binding instrument 'certain member states particularly those with a poor record will do nothing.' It also noted that increasing disparities between member states are directly contrary to Community aims of economic and social cohesion. (Pollock)

Community Social Charter

The Community Charter of Basic Social Rights for workers, adopted by all member states with the exception of the UK, addresses the social dimension of the European internal market and calls for measures to be developed to enable men and women to reconcile their work and family responsibilities.

It draws attention to the need for a Council of Ministers' decision on the Commission's proposed directive for parental leave. This would require member states to introduce statutory provision for a minimum of three months' parental leave for mothers and fathers. It also proposed a directive on the Protection of Pregnant Women at Work to include entitlement to 14 weeks of paid maternity leave for all women in employment.

Within the context of the social charter and in response to the examination of childcare provision and policies undertaken by the Network, the Commission has proposed a recommendation on childcare.

European Commission's Recommendation on Childcare

While the European Commission has so far failed to respond to the European Childcare Network's Recommendation of a directive on childcare, it has now adopted a recommendation (see below) which the Council of Ministers is expected to consider in December 1991. Such a recommendation would not be binding on member states. It might influence the general direction of childcare policies, but it would be unlikely in itself to trigger extensive developments in childcare services. However, the recommendation may be followed by a directive at a later stage given the support from the European Parliament's Women's Committee.

The Recommendation asks member states to develop measures in the following areas:

- to provide care for children while parents are in or seeking employment, education and training
- to develop leave arrangements for employed parents
- to make the environment, structure and organisation of the workplace responsive to the needs of workers with children
- to encourage the sharing of family responsibilities for the care and upbringing of children between women and men

Specific recommendations include:

Community services. The need for measures to enable 'all parents in employment, education and training to have equal access to locally based and high quality service'. Services should be affordable; combine safe and secure care with a broad education and pedagogical approach. Access to services should be determined by 'the needs of parents and children' and not only according to labour force requirements and should be equally available in all areas both urban and rural, Services should ensure access to children with special needs, with linguistic needs and to children in lone parent families.

Training of workers. Improvement of training (both initial and continuous) of workers in childcare services.

Community responsiveness. Services should be encouraged to work closely with local communities and with parents, and be responsive to local parental needs and circumstances. Recognition should be given to the role of public funding in the development of services although public funding could be supplemented by other sources of funding, for example, parents and employers.

Public funding. Member states should ensure that public funding makes an essential contribution to the development of affordable, good quality, coherent services which offer choice to parents.

Leave provision. Provision of leave enabling all employed parents, men and women, effectively to discharge their dual working and family responsibilities with appropriate levels of compensation for lost earnings, flexibility in the form of leave and appropriate length of leave.

Changes in workplace culture. Encouragement to employers and trade unions to make the environment, structure and organisation of the workplace supportive of the needs of all working parents.

European structural funding programme

The European Community's Structural Funds were reformed in 1988 to ensure that after the single European Act closer integration was accompanied by balanced social and economic development. The Fund's budget was substantially increased, and by 1993 will reach 14 billion ecus, doubling the real value from 1987. The revised objectives give more assistance to less developed regions, and improve the co-ordination of the Funds. The Funds comprise the European Regional Development Fund (ERDF), the European Social Fund (ESF) and the European Agricultural Guidance and Guarantee Fund, Guidance Section (EAGGF).

Major objectives of the Fund

- Promoting the development and structural adjustment of less developed regions
- Converting the regions seriously affected by industrial decline
- Combatting long-term unemployment
- Encouraging the integration of young people into employmen.
- Speeding up the adjustment of agricultural structures and promoting the development of rural areas

The role of childcare facilities has been recognised as contributing to a number of these objectives. A number of the Commission's own programmes, in particular the NOW initiative (a programme to provide New Opportunities for Women through employment and training measures) offer childcare facilities in disadvantaged areas, childcare to aid employment and training, and some financial support for childcare facilities and workers.

Since October 1989 a standard clause has been included in all Community Support Frameworks (five-year development plans) stipulating that consideration has to be given within programmes to 'training and infrastructure requirements which facilitate labour force participation by people with children.' Funding plans are prepared by government departments in partnership with local authorities, industrial training boards, educational establishments, voluntary organisations along with the TUC and CBI (Cohen, b).

Structural funding in relation to childcare is significant in a number of ways. Perhaps most important is the recognition of the economic impact of inadequacies in provision and of the role of childcare within economic development strategies. Some of the early applications for the use of the funds suggest the possibility of some interesting models.

Currently, only limited use has been made of these funding applications. For local authorities in the UK there is no clear support from government for using European funding in this area. In addition, at both local and national level, the relevance of childcare to the Fund objectives are ill-understood. However, European funding does offer the potential for an additional funding source for areas of greater need. Though potential is greatest in Northern Ireland, where childcare services can be funded as 'infrastructure', Fife Regional Council has also applied successfully for funds. It has received over £100,000 from the European Regional Development Fund towards the capital cost of its Partnership in Childcare scheme, and £21,000 from the European Social Fund. Other areas within Scotland, Wales and parts of rural England would also qualify for funding.

The funding applications identified for childcare illustrate the importance now attached by the European Commission to its economic significance. If the UK government were to give greater support to its use for these purposes, it could make a significant contribution to developing facilities in disadvantaged areas.

DEVELOPING A NATIONAL CHILDCARE POLICY

Having examined the evidence, we now turn to policy options and priorities. We suggest that policy-making should be based on the following principles.

Childcare is a key component of a modern welfare system

As we have seen, childcare has a vital role to play in enabling people to combine the responsibilities of parenthood with paid employment. It is especially important in helping mothers to achieve financial independence, which is probably the best way of protecting families from the hardship associated with lone parenthood, divorce and widowhood. At the same time, it is a central factor in enabling women to be educated, trained, employed and paid on an equal footing with men. Providing childcare is one of the most effective ways of relieving child poverty, as our cost-benefit analysis suggests (see Part Two); it has also been shown that children benefit in later life if they have had pre-school experience of being looked after and educated alongside other children.

Childcare can make a major contribution to the relief of disadvantage and to the promotion of equality. These goals are central to a modern welfare system. Childcare must therefore be seen not as an adjunct or afterthought, but as a key component of that system.

Childcare must serve a range of interests

A national childcare policy requires a comprehensive approach, which understands and encompasses its different functions. The following interests must be taken into account:

- **Parents:** to serve the interests of parents in general, but also to meet the distinctive needs of parents who are employed, those who are in education and training, and those who are not employed.
- **Children:** to serve the interests of children in general, but also to meet the distinctive needs of children in disadvantaged urban areas, those in rural areas and those with special requirements (ethnic, linguistic, or the special needs of children with disabilities).
- **Local communities:** to serve the interests of local communities, by trying to ascertain and accommodate the preferences of parents in the locality – minorities as well as majorities; also to help local

employers meet their childcare needs and to contribute to a useful infrastructure for the local economy.

- **The wider society:** to serve the longer-term social and economic interests of the country as a whole.

These points are elaborated below (p.60), when we consider the goals of a national childcare policy.

Provision must be equitable and responsive

We have said that one of the basic goals of a modern welfare system is to promote equality: this means not mean treating everyone the same, but giving everyone an equal chance in life. Childcare, as a key component of welfare, should be designed to ensure that, as far as possible, children and adults are equipped to participate in society, enjoy its fruits and realise their own potential. Yet this objective is based on an acknowledgement that people do not start out as equals. Policy must be geared to reducing disadvantages that are avoidable and compensating for those that are unavoidable.

Another major goal of welfare is to give ordinary people more control over their own lives ('empowerment'). Childcare intervenes at a fundamental level in people's living and working arrangements; it bears upon intimate familial relationships, as well as affecting the personal and economic opportunities of family members. For these reasons, childcare, more than than some other aspects of welfare, is one where people have widely varying requirements. A national policy should be flexible and responsive, to meet the need for childcare in a diversity of ways. It should also recognise that the goals of equity and responsiveness can conflict, and that planners and providers will have to negotiate between the two.

Childcare must encompass education and care

Childcare is a generic term, encompassing education, care and play. All three elements are important and can often be integrated. International reviews have increasingly focused on the need for an integrated approach to education and care, 'educare', and more generally for improved co-ordination of all services.

The UK government has been concerned to improve standards of day nurseries, and this was made evident in the 1989 Children Act. However, a government report on the quality of educational experience, *Starting with Quality*, restricted its enquiry to three and four year olds. By contrast, countries such as Denmark, Spain and Italy have been developing a more educational approach to children under three in nurseries.

Commitment to an integrated approach would have significant implications for policy development, affecting administrative responsibilities, political direction and the practical development of services. Two immediate concerns are for day nurseries to have a sound educational element, and for nursery schools and classes to meet the care needs of children and parents. Ultimately, the aim should be to remove the distinction between these forms of childcare.

Policies on childcare and employment provision must be linked

The way people use childcare services, and what they demand of them, depends to a large extent on whether they have jobs and, if so, on their entitlements to take time off, paid or unpaid. For instance, a mother may be unable to take advantage of her entitlement to return to work after a period of maternity leave if she cannot make suitable childcare arrangements; or she may be obliged to make childcare arrangements (suitable or otherwise) before she is ready to return to work, because her period of leave has run out. These two forms of provision are so closely linked that it is essential for policies to be developed in tandem.

Childcare can pay economic as well as social dividends

The fact that childcare has an economic as well as a social dimension has been a common thread running through recent international reviews of childcare policy. For example, a 1988 study for the Australian government was based on two propositions. First, society has interests in the well-being of children, which go beyond individual parents' interests. Second, the direct costs of purchasing childcare are much higher than those incurred by individual parents (almost always women) who stay at home and do it themselves: this heavily discourages women's entry into the labour force (Cass).

An 1986 Canadian study similarly examined not only social benefits (such as improvements in early child development) but such factors as job creation arising from childcare programmes, increased income tax revenues and increased consumer spending (Townson).

There are two important implications for policy-making:

- **Public interest:** this encompasses not only the social requirements of children and their parents, as well as the wider community, but also the needs of the community for an efficient labour market and a prosperous economy.

- **Public funding:** this should be seen not only as social expenditure, to meet welfare needs, but also as a sound investment, contributing to economic development.

Our cost benefit analysis (p.93) shows the economic as well as the social benefits which can accrue from a substantial increase in public investment in childcare.

What should a national childcare policy seek to achieve?

Having set out the guiding principles for a national child care policy, the next step is to establish more detailed objectives. What should a national childcare policy seek to achieve - for children, for women, for men and for the country as a whole?

For children

- Access to the social, educational and long-term economic benefits which can be derived from pre-school care and education, to help all children grow towards responsible adult citizenship.

- Services delivered irrespective of parental income, disability or ethnic background.

- Stability and continuity in the combination of home-based parental care and group-based 'nursery' provision - avoiding a multiplicity of *ad hoc* arrangements.

- Childcare services provided by adequately trained and properly paid workers; low staff turnover, secure staff/child relationships, and high standards of care and education.

- Access to a period of full-time care by mothers and fathers; high standards of care at home, whether from parents, care workers (nannies) or other relatives.

- Support (as appropriate) for children's cultural and linguistic identities.

- Help for families to achieve adequate standards of living, so that no child lives in poverty.

For women

- Access to education, training and employment which will enable them to participate as workers and as citizens on an equal footing with men.
- Employment provisions which enable them to combine paid work and active parenthood, including maternity, parental and family leave, and flexibility in working hours and arrangements.
- Services and employment provisions which take account of the needs of all women, especially lone mothers, those who have children with special needs and women with specific cultural and linguistic requirements
- Opportunities to achieve and sustain financial independence while combining family responsibilities and paid work; life-time earning capacity and retirement income to be unaffected by the decision to have a child; financial independence to be such that it diminishes the economic impact of divorce, widowhood and old age.
- Adequate pay and conditions for childcare workers, most of whom are women and currently poorly paid.
- Men to share the responsibilities of parenthood on an equal footing with women.

For men

- Conditions which enable them to be actively involved in the care of their children; suitable employment provisions including paid leave for childcare and other family responsibilities, and flexible working arrangements.
- Providers of childcare services and employers to recognise and support men's role in caring for children.
- Opportunities for employment in childcare services.

For families

- Improve the quality of life for families; strengthen the family as a social unit by recognising and supporting the child care needs of all its members.

For the economy

- Removal of barriers and disincentives to women entering and remaining in the labour market on an equal footing with men.
- Better access for parents (especially mothers) to education and training, to increase the supply of skilled labour.
- Better use to be made of existing skills in the population.
- Create new jobs and strengthen infrastructures, to assist economic development.
- Enhance the potential of the future labour force.

The case for public responsibility

Taking account of the principles and objectives outlined above, there is an overwhelming case for childcare being a matter of public responsibility. That is not to say that responsibility rests solely in the public domain: as we explain below, parents, families, local groups, voluntary organisations, employers and trade unions all have a part to play. But it is up to the government to take the lead responsibility, by setting out and implementing a national childcare policy. The diversity and breadth of public interest represented by the objectives require a correspondingly broad definition of public responsibility.

The current definition of public responsibility for childcare in the UK is narrow and (in some areas) uncertain. In practice, it has been diminished to that of a residual provider, an over-stretched and underfunded regulator, and a limited promoter of the voluntary and burgeoning private sector.

As far as employment provisions are concerned, minimal entitlements in relation to pregnancy and maternity reflect a partial acknowledgement of public responsibility in this area. However, as we have seen, provisions are entirely inadequate and the White Paper, *Building Businesses not Barriers*, proposes that they be further diminished. The UK government has entered reservations in relation to the relevant articles of the UN Convention on Women; it has taken no action to extend provision in line with policy developments at EC level.

The inadequacy of this definition has been underlined by demographic and employment changes, by the views of expert bodies in the UK, and by EC and international opinion. For example:

- The Equal Opportunities Commission states: 'Women cannot enjoy genuine equality of opportunity unless they have access to daycare facilities for their children. The complete inadequacy of current provision for both the under-fives and dependent school age children is now probably one of the most important factors restricting many women's opportunities'. (EOC 1990)
- The National Children's Bureau states: 'Central and local government have a duty, working in partnership with parents, to ensure that services and support are available for families; services that encourage children's cognitive, social, emotional and physical development; and meet parents' need for support for themselves and for daycare for their children.' (National Children's Bureau)
- A Recommendation on Childcare recently adopted by the European Commission and to be considered by the Council of Ministers in December 1991, specifies that member states should be responsible for ensuring equitable access to services and employment provisions for parents in paid employment, education and training. The UK government rejects the idea of legislation on parental leave and has blocked the EC's proposed Directive on that issue. It has also opposed, for similar reasons, the recently proposed EC Directive on the Protection at Work of Pregnant Women.
- The United Nations Convention on the Elimination of All Forms of Discrimination against Women, specifies in Article 112(c) that state parties should encourage the provision of necessary supporting social services to enable parents to combine family obligations with work responsibilities and participation in public life; in particular, it says, they should promote the establishment and development of a network of childcare facilities. Article 18(3) of the UN Convention on the Rights of the Child specifies that state parties 'should take all appropriate measures to ensure that children of working parents have the right to benefit from children's services and facilities for which they are eligible'.

Public responsibility, expressed in terms of a national childcare policy, requires a local and a national dimension. At a national level, it must involve several government departments (Health, Education, Environment, Industry, Employment). It also demands a strong lead from a single cabinet-level department, to co-ordinate an overall strategy, and to ensure that it is implemented.

Family and community share responsibility with government

Public responsibility lies in providing a national policy and developing a framework within which agreed objectives can be met. The implementation of policy entails sharing responsibilities with family and community. The public policy framework must take account of the potential and the limitations of all parties involved.

- **Families.** Responsibilities are shared primarily with parents, or with others who are parent figures in a child's life. They are, of course, the ones who are chiefly responsible for bringing up and caring for children. Their responsibility carries with it substantive rights for parents/guardians in determining the nature of care for their child. Nevertheless, it should be placed within a framework of public support. This should take account of changing patterns of family life and particularly of the way in which over-reliance on family-based care can affect the lives of women (Finch). It should also recognise that children have some needs which cannot easily be met by their families alone.

- **Voluntary organisations.** Some of the larger national charities have assumed shared responsibility for meeting the requirements of children in need. Other voluntary organisations have assumed extensive responsibility for providing more general childcare services, mainly by promoting self-help activities such as the playgroup movement.

  In general, the great strength of voluntary organisations has been their ability to identify needs unmet elsewhere and to set up 'demonstration' projects, as models for others to follow. They have thus helped to develop new forms of provision - for example, community nurseries and networks offering advice and advocacy. But how far should they get involved in mainstream provision of childcare services? One difficulty arises over the use of money raised through charitable giving for services which many believe ought to be provided out of public funds. Another problem is that most charitable bodies are geared towards provision for disadvantaged children; unless they can broaden their approach, they may compound the problem of stigmatising childcare by restricting access to the 'needy'. A further difficulty is that if their energies are channelled into providing regular services, or if their activities become too closely controlled by government, their capacity for innovation and experiment could be stifled - and this could be a loss to the childcare system as a whole. They require a framework of public support which does not seek to turn them into mainstream providers of volume services, but which maintains their independence and their ability to come up with new and diverse forms of care.

- **Local groups.** Groups based in the community have responded to local requirements by setting up childcare services. Because they are close to the families involved, they tend to be well-attuned to their needs and preferences. They usually involve parents in running services - in management groups, and/or directly as paid or unpaid care workers. Sometimes these groups are under the auspices of larger voluntary organisations; often they are not.

One great advantage of local groups is that they can harness otherwise untapped resources: the energy, experience, time and commitment of local people. Another is that they retain control over decisions (for instance, about what kind of services to provide, and for whom) within communities and among parents. They can also contribute to the local political system, by representing the views of particular groups and lobbying elected authorities.

However, a service run by and for local parents may operate an exclusive admittance policy (for example, refusing children with special needs, or those from other ethnic groups). Their practices are even harder to monitor and regulate than those of larger voluntary organisations. Their resources are often severely limited, so that they may have inadequate facilities, untrained personnel, and lack the means to provide education as well as care. Their use of volunteer or cheap labour may be exploitative, unless time is offered willingly by individuals (and they are usually women) who have chosen freely to do such work. Activities based on the principles of self-help and mutual aid can be empowering, but they can also be disempowering if they trap people into low-paid or unpaid, time-consuming activities which prevent them taking up other opportunities. Over-reliance on local groups for childcare has particular implications for women as consumers, volunteers and workers.

As with larger voluntary organisations, local groups need public support which encourages them to provide services compatible with public policy, but does not impose undue control which could undermine their enthusiasm or creativity.

- **Employers.** The government has increasingly stressed employers' responsibility to provide for working parents. In 1989 this policy was signalled within the five-point plan of the ministerial group on women's issues which included 'more encouragement for employers to use existing tax relief to provide childcare'. The following year the government finally stopped taxing employees for nursery places subsidised by their employers.

  Employers do have a significant interest in childcare being available to their employees. However, there are several reasons why they should not be expected to bear that responsibility single-handedly. Childcare should be organised to serve a range of interests, not just those of employers and employees; there is a danger that employer-provided care could produce a 'tied cottage' effect, rendering employees vulnerable to exploitation. Smaller and less profitable areas of employment could find the burden of paying for childcare threatens their survival. Last but not least, if employment provisions such as maternity and parental leave, are to be developed as part of a national childcare policy (as we argue they should), this gives employers another major area of responsibility. As far as childcare services are concerned, public policy should concentrate on establishing a dialogue with employers, involving them where possible in developing facilities; it should encourage them to help financially, but should not oblige all employers to foot a substantial portion of the bill.

- **Trade unions.** When it comes to promoting a work-place culture more responsive to the demands of families, trade unions share responsibility with employers. The trade union movement has for some years consistently pointed to the need for goverments to accept responsibility for providing childcare and has for some time been encouraging union negotiators to include childcare on their bargaining agenda. The TUC has called for 'an expansion of state provision to European levels' (Cohen, 1990). It is worth noting here that the Australian trade union movement helped secure broad political support for the programme of social security reform and public funding for childcare services which has formed part of the Australian programmme to combat child poverty.

The role of government

We have argued that government should take the lead responsibility for a national childcare policy. This does not mean it will provide all services directly. There are three main functions for governement:

- to promote the provision of services and to provide funds;
- to ensure adequate standards of provision, so that services and that they meet the needs of children, families and communities;
- to promote and fund the development of employment provisions for working parents.

We look first at the question of funding childcare, to see which measures are likely to be most effective in pursuing the principles and goals outlined above.

Funding child care

Public expenditure on childcare services in this country has not increased significantly over the last ten years and is substantially lower than a number of European countries, most notably Denmark which is spending approximately six or seven times as much on services for under-fives as the UK (Cohen, 1990; CEC, a). This has not been a low-cost option but an allocation of the costs to others. The issue is not 'whether we can afford the costs because they already exist, but how these costs are allocated, in particular between parents, employers and society' (CEC, a). Furthermore, there are heavy long-term costs involved in failing to commit public funds to childcare. These costs are born by women, by children, by childcare workers and by employers. There are also, as we show below (see Part Two), significant costs for government, in terms of tax revenues forgone and expenditure on social security benefits.

Public funding can take a variety of forms; it can involve giving money to parents to spend on childcare (demand subsidies) or funding services (supply subsidies), or a combination of both.

Demand subsidies

Tax relief

This is one form of demand subsidy which has been extensively canvassed: tax relief on child care expenses incurred by parents - that is, money paid by parents for child care should be exempt from taxation. The advantages of tax relief, which are shared by most forms of demand subsidy, include:

- stimulating the development of facilities by helping parents to pay;
- enabling parents to choose between services;
- discouraging the hidden economy in childcare, because payments must be declared before they can attract tax relief.

It has also been argued that tax relief helps to improve the pay and conditions of childcare workers, although there is no clear evidence for this. The disadvantages of tax relief include:

- helping only those with income above the tax threshold and (if tax is deducted above the base rate) favouring higher-income families;
- covering only a small proportion of the costs (eg. if the parent paid £100 per week and paid tax at 25 per cent, the subsidy would amount to £25, or a quarter of the total);
- no direct contribution to equitable access or quality of services;
- encourages *ad hoc* provision, rather than the development of a comprehensive service for all;
- may inflate the cost of childcare, increasing the difficulties of lower income groups.

Childcare credits and vouchers

If tax relief for childcare were combined with a childcare benefit or 'tax credit' for parents below the tax threshold, this would overcome some of the disadvantages of tax relief, in that better-off parents would no longer be favoured. The idea of tax credits has been mooted for some time, as part of proposals for an integrated tax and social security system. It would, however, carry the danger of inflating the cost of childcare, as it lacks the advantage of supply-side investment, which can influence directly the phasing-in of services together with the necessary infrastructure, including training. Like tax relief, it makes no direct contribution to the equitable access or quality of services and encourages *ad hoc* provision rather than the development of a comprehensive service which makes effective use of existing resources.

As a variation on this theme, there have been proposals for a public childcare 'voucher': cash paid by the state to parents, to help cover their childcare costs. There are different views about whether it should be available to all parents who wanted to make childcare arrangements, or only to those deemed to be 'in need'. If it were subject to a means-test it would raise the problem of whether to test both parents' income, or only that of the parent (usually the mother) with primary responsibility for childcare; it would also compound the effects of the 'poverty trap'. It could create considerable hardship for parents in precarious employment, where time elapses between changes in their entitlement and receipt of benefit. If vouchers were available to all, they would, like tax credits, be either extremely costly and an inefficient use of public money, or too small to make an impact on most families' childcare options. Better-off families would be able to top-up vouchers to buy the care they needed and the rest would have little or no choice. The government would be spending considerable sums of money, without any control over the nature or quality of care available to families.

Some employers pay to employees with childcare responsibilities childcare cheques or vouchers (rather like luncheon vouchers). There is a small financial advantage to the employer in paying out money this way, but for the employee the voucher is regarded as taxable income. In some cases, vouchers can be tied to a particular service (as with childminder vouchers) or redeemed against a specified range of services. They are worth the same to all who receive them but are more likely to be available in certain areas of employment. Vouchers which are tied to a particular service deprive parents of choice, while both these and more flexible options may have a 'tied cottage' effect, leaving parents without the option of changing jobs.

Fee relief

This is a variant of demand subsidy involving payments directly to childcare services to enable them to reduce or remove fees from low-income families. This form of subsidy is used extensively in Australia and Canada, where it is combined with supply subsidies in the form of capital and operational grants.

Fee relief is appropriate in a system where parents are expected to make some contribution to childcare costs, and where services are intended to be available on something approaching an equitable basis (ie. without excluding or penalising poorer families). It helps poorer families without providing for them in segregated services which may become stigmatised. Unlike tax relief, it concentrates help among low-income families. In Australia approximately 12 per cent of families using publicly funded childcare in 1988 had incomes below A$14,000 per annum and 70 per cent below A$32,000. Thirty-five per cent of children used services for reasons other than their parents' employment and many of these were from special needs groups (Brennan and Stonehouse).

Used in conjunction with other public subsidies, fee relief has contributed in Australia to a very significant expansion in childcare places. These increased from 46,000 in 1983 to 122,000 in 1990. It is estimated that they will increase to 192,000 places in 1994/5 (Brennan and Stonehouse; Cass). The figures include childcare places for school-age children, out of school hours. The Australian programme is seen as increasingly offering parents a choice between different forms of care: centre or family based, at the workplace, or in the local neighbourhood (Brennan and Stonehouse).

Two main difficulties associated with fee relief are

- how parents should be assessed as eligible for fee relief
- for which types of childcare parents can claim it.

Should parents be assessed on the basis of needs or on the basis of income? Eligibility testing is always problematic. How should tests be administered, by which authorities and who should decide upon the criteria? It can be complicated and costly to administer; it can be unduly intrusive for those who are tested; it can be hard to ensure fair decision-making. Income-testing raises awkward questions about whose income should be taken into account, and at what income levels parents should become eligible. Like all means-tested benefits, it is almost bound to deter some parents from going out to work, or from pursuing higher pay. The worst effects of this 'poverty trap' can be offset by having a higher threshold for eligibility - but that of course puts a greater financial burden on the public purse. Simpler tests are easier and cheaper to administer, but they are cruder in their arbitrations and may be less than fair to some parents.

In Australia income testing for fee relief is combined with needs-based principles in prioritising access to places. In the Canadian province of Ontario a proposed switch from needs testing to income testing was seen as a move to a 'simpler, less intrusive system for eligibility screening' (Ministry of Community and Social Services, Ontario).

The second main difficulty with fee relief is whether it should be available for all forms of provision, or only for selected ones. Countries operating fee relief generally restrict its use to services provided through nurseries or daycare centres; fee relief for childminders or nannies has never been considered a serious opiton. But should fee relief be available for parents who use private, profit-making child-care? Or should be it restricted to services provided by publicly-owned or other not-for-profit organisations?

In Australia fee relief was initially only available to non-profit services but it has recently been extended (controversially) to the commercial sector. In Canada there have been mixed policies on providing subsidies to the profit sector and considerable criticism within some provinces over the extent to which this has contributed to the development of the commercial childcare sector. As a result of funding changes in some areas, commercial day nursery provision is now diminishing in Canada as a proportion of total day nursery provision (Pence in Cochran ed).

One argument against fee relief for profit-making services is that public funds should not be used (even partly or indirectly) for private gain; they would be better spent on services where all revenues were devoted to expanding and/or improving provision. Another argument is that profit-making services tend to drive not-for-profit services out of the market - for a variety of reasons: they use aggressive marketing techniques, or they pay exploitative wages, or they find it easier to acquire capital. Once they have achieved a dominant market position, they are likely to drive up costs. And if their primary interest is in profitability, they may pursue economic efficiency at the expense of quality services. The experience of the United States healthcare market is salutory: provision is based on commercial principles, costs have escalated out of control, many of the providers have amassed considerable personal wealth, and many patients have suffered from grossly inequitable services and poor outcomes. In the Canadian province of Ontario when (prior to 1987) similar public funding was available to commercial and not-for-profit childcare centres, wages in the commercial sector were on average 30 per cent lower than the not-for-profit sector and 50 per cent lower than in the public sector. Similar evidence is available from other Canadian provinces (Ontario Coalition for Better Childcare).

Against these arguments, it can be said that any national childcare policy will have to build on what exists, and private providers are already there; if government wants to increase the number of childcare places within reasonable time limits, it cannot afford to withold support from the private sector. Certainly, in Australia, the decision to extend fee relief to private childcare was taken because government saw this as the best way meeting urgent demands for childcare places. It may be argued that some in the private sector are less interested in making substantial profits than in simply earning a living and providing useful services: this particularly applies to small private nurseries and to most childminders (and nannies).

Fee relief can constitute a larger or smaller part of the government's demand subsidy to childcare, depending on levels of supply subsidies. It can also play a greater or lesser role in enhancing parental choice, depending on how much it is worth to parents and on what conditions it is granted to them.

The market approach to childcare

In general, demand subsidies involve a market approach to the delivery of childcare services. On their own, they cannot ensure that all parents' needs are met, nor respond to children with special needs. Nor can they easily respond to the particular difficulties of delivering services in rural or disadvantaged urban areas. And whilst it is frequently argued that this approach allows more choice it tends to produce a pattern of services which do not reflect what we know of parental preferences. For example, the most significant expansion in private sector services over recent years has been in the form of individual care givers.

Services for the under-threes are considerably more expensive to provide, requiring more staff and more space. This diminishes the opportunity for profit, and has contributed to the development of a private childcare sector predominantly based on childminders and nannies, alongside the large informal sector involving family and friends. Childminders may be a preferred option of some parents for their younger children (for example, for those under two), but their current use for older pre-school children does not in general reflect expressed parental preference. As far as private nurseries are concerned, Penn's recent survey notes that a great many are in a precarious financial situation which threatens their continuing existence, and that the overwhelming majority caters for professional or middle to high income earners (Penn).

In the United States, this market approach to childcare has led to what has been described as 'a patch work of daycare . . . leaving many holes and uneven coverage' (Phillips in Melhuish and Moss).

For all these reasons, demand subsidies by themselves do not appear to constitute an effective strategy for developing childcare in line with the objectives we have set out. They have attracted little support from recent examinations of childcare policy. The Equal Opportunities Commision of Great Britain concludes that 'more and better childcare would meet the needs of children, parents and employers much more effectively then tax deductions of childcare costs' and also firmly rejects the possibility reintroducing child tax allowances either to replace or accompany child benefit. (EOC 1990) The most recent European Childcare Network report notes that only four European countries provide tax relief for childcare and in all cases it is provided alongside other policies aimed at increasing publicly funded services. The report concludes that 'demand subsidy is not a satisfactory long-term strategy for funding a range of childcare services proposed in this report. (CEC, a).

We discuss later the way in which demand subsidies may be combined with other forms of public support (p.87).

Supply subsidies

Government can subsidise the supply-side of childcare in two main ways: by providing services itself (principally through local authorities) and by funding non-government providers.

Publicly provided services

As we have seen, in those EC countries which offer the highest levels of childcare, services have mainly been provided by public authorities or through independent organisations run on a similar basis. In the UK, most pre-school educational services are delivered by local authorities. Where day nurseries are concerned, the role of local authorities has diminished, but they remain the principal providers of services aimed at meeting the welfare requirements of children and families.

These services are open to criticism, for ghettoising disadvantaged children, for being slow to respond to the changing needs of families, for being pitifully under-resourced, and generally for failing to pursue the objectives we have outlined here. This is principally due to the failure of government to provide a strong and coherent policy framework and to back this up with the necessary financial support.

Public service models for the delivery of childcare have three main advantages. First, they are able to be more consistent in the use of trained staff, access to support services, and offering reasonable pay and conditions - all key elements in ensuring continuity and quality of care. Secondly, they are better at delivering volume services in a consistent manner, without unnecessary duplication of development work or of services. Thirdly, their services are generally easier to monitor, regulate and evaluate.

These advantages point to a substantial role for local authorities in delivering services, to include:

- Day nurseries and centres which combine the functions of care and education. These would be open to a range of children: they would neither exclude, nor exclusively provide for children with designated welfare needs. They could be provided directly by local authorities, or in partnership with other agencies, including community organisations, employers, education and training establishments and local development agencies.

- A framework of support and regulation for home-based childcare, including direct employment of childminders and linked where possible to centre-based care. This kind of service has been developed extensively in Denmark and France but as yet there are only isolated examples in the UK, where in general systems for registering self-employed childminders offer minimal support and little or no flexibility. Such schemes would improve the quality of care by developing a better-trained and motivated workforce, with a lower turnover of staff and greater continuity for families. They could provide a useful option for parents of younger children, help with care for sick children, assist with treatment programmes for disabled children and act as a flexible resource - for parents with occasional childcare requirements, as well as to back up the welfare function of nurseries. They could be undertaken by local authorities themselves or in partnership with others.

- Pre-school education services which also meet parental requirements of care. These could involve extended-hour schemes for nursery schools and classes, as well as the development of centres (possibly in partnership with other agencies), offering integrated services for all under-fives, or a wider range of provision, including family daycare and informal services, such as mother and toddler groups.

- Childcare services for school-age children, offering opportunities to participate in a range of educational and recreational activities. As with services for the under-fives, these should not be regarded as having simply a 'minding' function and should meet the needs of all children including those with special needs. Services could be within or outside schools and could be developed by authorities themselves and/or by community organisations and other agencies. Voluntary and community organisations could be involved in determining what form provision should take and in examining the range of activities to be available.

- Education authorities should be given statutory reponsibilities to consider care as well as educational requirements in relation to school hours, school meals and school transport; they should have a duty to provide directly within school hours, and to provide directly, or to secure from other agencies services outside normal school hours. This responsiblity should in principle relate to all children up to the age of 14 and to children with special needs up to 19, but is most immediately pressing for children under the age of 11.

Publicly Funded Services

Public support for childcare can take the form of financial and other assistance for non-government providers. These fall into two main categories:

- not-for-profit, including voluntary organisations and local groups;

- profit-making, including large and small private nurseries (owned individually or in chains); self-employed childminders and private nannies.

The main advantages of funding non-government providers apply chiefly to the not-for-profit sector, where public support

- encourages diverse forms of provision
- taps resources (human and material) that would not be available to state-run services
- speeds the development of services, helping to make more places available sooner
- helps to identify gaps in state provision
- stimulates provision in areas which are relatively hard for government to reach, particularly rural areas and in communities with particular linguistic and cultural requirements.

The main difficulties are that non-government providers may be less committed to an integrated and equitable approach (often understandably, as where local groups provide for their own children); they may also be harder to monitor and regulate - because of their diversity, and because of their distance from the state. On balance, the advantages substantially outweigh the difficulties, although there are particular problems related to profit-making services which we have already discussed (p.72). In the context of a national childcare policy, publicly-funded services should be seen as complementary to publicly-provided services, and be developed alongside them; they cannot be regarded as the main source of volume services.

Funding could include:

- Public grants to parent groups and community organisations, using this strategy to extend services in areas which are 'hard to reach' and to help meet particular linguistic and cultural requirements. These could include formal and informal services.
- Grants to help community groups and voluntary agencies develop partnership schemes (see below), where the local authority does not want to take on the initiating role.
- Funding training and support services for voluntary schemes, as well as for individual care givers not employed by local authorities, and possibly also for private nurseries (we discuss the public funding of private sector childcare below).
- Grants, as appropriate, to organisations providing information and advocacy schemes.

Examples of public funding strategies

In the UK, the Greater London Council (now defunct) pioneered the extensive funding of non-government schemes, to meet the needs of groups not effectively provided for by public authorities. The GLC's funding programme stimulated the development of parent- and community-run nurseries, some notable for their exemplary equal opportunities practices, and for meeting minority language requirements.

In a number of EC countries, public funding has been used to support projects initiatied by voluntary organisations and local groups. Notably in Denmark and France, public funding strategies over recent years have supported schemes developed and managed by communities and parent groups, as a means of extending services into rural areas in a culturally appropriate forms. In both countries these measures are part of a national strategy which includes extensive public provision. In Denmark, government grants have enabled groups of parents to start and run their own services. In France, agreements between local and national authourities to fund and develop services have been extended to include voluntary associations as local partners, reflecting the increasing strength of parent-led initiatives; local employers may also be included as partners. (Combes in Cochran, ed; SCAFA).

In Canada and Australia, a range of public subsidies has been used in conjuction with capital funding to increase provision. In New Zealand, public funding in the form of operational grants are available to all early childhood care and education services providing for children up to five, irrespective of the nature of provider or form of service. Public funding provides for up to ten half-day sessions a week for each child enrolled, with the intention of bringing funding of all early childhood services to the same level as Kindergarten. Funding is subject to a charter agreed with the Ministery of Education, outlining aims, objectives and curriculum, and subject to the agreement of parents using or likely to use the service. Funding arrangements were initially tied to the use of qualified staff. This is now not required, although national agreements on salary scales for recognised qualifications have to be observed. Non-profit services are given priority for capital funding, which is available through discretionary grants. Full capital costs are met only in exceptional cases, and involve transfer of property to the Crown. All pre-five services have been made the responsibility of the Ministry of Education, as part of a strong emphasis on integrated care and education. (Smith; May).

The New Zealand model reflects a widely perceived need in that country for a community development approach, to take particular account of the substantial minority living within rural areas and the needs of the Maori population. In the early stages of the scheme, the funding of for-profit services presented problems of accountability; in general, concern has been expressed over funding levels and whether conditions attached to funding provide sufficient quality control. But it is as yet too early to assess the effects of the New Zealand reforms.

Public funding for the voluntary sector. A structure of services which depends too heavily upon parental and communuity action may encourage unequal provision, favour communities with a greater capacity for organisation and in some cases involve duplication of efforts and services. However, the use of this form of funding strategy to supplement public services does offer a means of enabling parents and other community groups to shape provision to meet their needs, and of providing local authorities with insights into gaps in their own services. This has long been a recognised role for the voluntary sector; within childcare both community nurseries and pre-school playgroups have influenced public sector provision in relation to parent management and parent participation within services. It is an approach which could encompass centre and family daycare as well as more informal services.

The criteria for funding voluntary organisations and local groups should be guided by the objectives set out in this report. As far as possible, grants should depend upon the recipient organisations meeting specified conditions about the nature and quality of care, as well as about their employment practices. But criteria should be developed sensitively and with sufficient flexibility to ensure that the strengths of the voluntary sector (its capacity to identify unmet needs, to involve individuals and groups in the community in planning and delivery, to innovate, experiment and campaign for change) is not undermined.

Public funding for the private sector. We have discussed the main arguments against a market approach to childcare. The question remains of how far the disadvantages of this approach can be mitigated by public policy in general, and by public funding in particular. Demand subsidies such as tax relief on childcare expenses can do litle to influence patterns of provision in the private sector. Fee relief would offer greater (though still limited) opportunities for influencing provision, if it were made available only for approved schemes which met specifications in line with national objectives; this might also be true of a public childcare voucher scheme, in which vouchers could be 'cashed in' only with designated providers. Supply subsidies can influence patterns of provision more directly.

Even with a substantial expansion of other services it is probable that self-employed childminders and nannies will continue to be a significant form of care. In Denmark, private childminders still care for eight per cent of children, although publicly-employed childminders now care for twice as many. Nannies are the oldest form of childcare (outside family care) and will undoubtedly continue to be employed by some families. Public funds could usefully be spent on providing better training and access to support services for these care workers and, in addition, on providing advice and information services for parents.

Many private nurseries have considerable training needs and funding should be available to facilitate their access to training. Such tax assistance as is currently available to private sector providers could be continued. However, there is less justification for direct funding for private, for-profit services - whether by means of fee relief or in the form of capital or operational grants. Where public funds are limited, choices have to be made about how to spend them: we take the view that, in the context of a national childcare policy, public funds would be better invested in not-for-profit services, for reasons we have already explored. In general, for-profit services can be seen as a way of helping to bridge the gap between demand and supply, and of adding to the range of provision; they cannot be seen as a source of volume services within the context of a national childcare policy.

The advantages of partnership

Over recent years an increasing number of local authorities have examined ways of developing services in partnership with other agencies - for example, community organisations, employers (public and private), education and training establishments, and local development agencies. To date, the number of schemes has been few, reflecting difficulties in resourcing, absence of specific encouragement from government and, in some cases, difficulties co-ordinating between potential partners.

Partnership offers an appropriate model for tapping resources available from the European Community's stuctural funds, particularly in areas of industrial decline and in some rural areas. In Scotland, for example, Fife Regional Council has developed a partnership programme for childcare, which has attracted EC funds.

It has several other advantages. Partnership schemes embrace a range of interests and thereby encourage a broader perspective on what constitutes a satisfactory childcare scheme. This can be particularly helpful in rural areas, where the viability of a scheme may depend on it combining several functions. Partnership promotes more effective use of resources - for example, by ensuring that facilities based in colleges are used throughout the year. It also provides a forum for local authorities to discuss with employers and other partners ways of developing better conditions for working parents and more child-friendly environments.

Ensuring quality childcare

Government has a key role to play in ensuring that childcare services are consistent with national objectives and meet the needs of local communities. This entails:

- understanding and responding to local needs
- setting standards and measuring performance
- promoting parental choice
- training childcare workers and promoting good employment practices
- regular review and inspection.

Responding to local needs. Local government should be responsible for finding out the particular needs of local communities. Planning should be based on sound information about local needs and, where possible, local people should be involved in decision-making. The model of local service agreements, pioneered by Islington, York and other local authorities, could be adapted for the development of childcare (Pfeffer and Coote, 53).

The planning and co-ordination of local services would require appropriate mechanisms within local authorities (such as co-ordinating committees for childcare), improved statistics on local conditions and population trends, up-to-date information on existing provision, regular reviews of parental demands and preferences, and access to research and information on models of good childcare practice.

Voluntary organisations and local groups have an important role to play in eliciting and representing the views of local people, analysing trends and demands, establishing unmet consumer needs and promoting good practice. Local authority grants to local groups to develop and run childcare schemes themselves will also help to encourage responsive services.

Once schemes are in operation, the involvement of parents in managing them will help to make them more responsive. Training for parents and advocacy schemes will help to strengthen this kind of involvement.

Setting standards. Central government should set standards for childcare, to encourage provision consistent with national objectives. These standards should be clear and rigorously enforced, but they should also be minimal, to allow for diversity, innovation and experiment; local authorities should be able to develop their own guidelines, based on national standards and taking account of local needs and conditions. Public funds should be conditional upon providers meeting these standards; they could be allowed to do so in stages, over an agreed period to ease the development of new projects. Funding authorities should take responsibility for ensuring that services are regularly monitored and evaluated; funds for all childcare schemes (public and independent) should include enough money to pay for these essential processes.

Promoting choice. Choice is often equated with variety, but diversity does not in itself guarantee choice. Consumer choice is currently severely constrained by the shortage of satisfactory services - although the services that exist are fairly diverse. The limited but significant role of choice in promoting quality is discussed in another IPPR report (Pfeffer and Coote). Public funding of non-government providers (especially local groups) will encourage diversity and possibly also choice, as the volume of provision increases. But diversity should be developed within the context of national standards and alongside strategies aimed at promoting equitable services.

That said, all parents should be able to choose to make the following arrangements for their children:

- Satisfactory standards of group care, including day nurseries, for children under three.

- More formal educational provision integrated with care for three- and four-year-olds.
- Less formal provision for play/social interaction of children and parents.
- Care by an individual care giver in the worker's or the parents' own home.
- Parental care facilitated through employment provisions including parental leave and access to flexible working arrangements.

The most extensive choice is needed for parents of children under three where the evidence shows that preferences are more diverse than among parents of three to five year olds. Choice should also be promoted to take account of cultural and linguistic requirements, and of parents' preferences for work- or community-based provision. For school children it might be argued that there should be choice between recreationally based and educationally based activities although this choice could be offered within the same facility.

Training and employment practices. 'Good quality services require recruitment and retention of good quality workers, which in turn requires levels of training, pay and conditions that reflect the importance, demands and complexity of the work. This in turn will bring increased status, revaluing what has become devalued work.' (EC Childcare Network, d).

Quality in the delivery of childcare services depends to a large extent upon the skills and commitment of the workforce. We have stressed the importance of training for all childcare workers: nursery staff, childminders and nannies. Training should include initial and in-service courses. We have also pointed to the way in which wages and conditions of childcare workers affect staff morale and turnover, and hence the stability and quality of children's experience. Public support for childcare should include sufficient funds for training and career development, for decent pay and conditions, and for the promotion of equal opportunities in recruitment and promotion of staff. This should apply to publicly-funded as well as to publicly provided services.

Review and inspection. Effective mechanisms are required for assessing childcare services on a regular basis. Local authorities should carry out regular reviews of parents' demands and preferences, and how far these are met by existing services. HMIs and local education authority advisors provide an inspection mechanism at national and local level which could be extended to cover a wider range of services. They require more effective support through an adequately funded research programme and improved information gathering on all services.

Funding 'quality'. It should be stressed that all these processes cost money. It is essential that public funds are made available for gathering information, carrying out research, consulting the public and involving local people in decision making; for regulation, monitoring and evaluation; for training and good employment practices; for review and inspection.

Innovations and good practice

One important means of pursuing quality is to identify and spread good practice. Although in general provision is severely limited, there are nevertheless model schemes which suggest what can be achieved. Here we describe briefly just a few childcare schemes in the UK and elsewhere in Europe which provide examples of good practice.

Manchester City Council has opened six children's centres; six more are planned. These offer free full-time/part-time and sessional care for children aged six months and over. The centres provide for children on a neighbourhood basis and offer in addition to day nursery facilities, facilities for school-age children, informal parent and toddlers and play sessions. The City Council is now offering some places to employers as a means of extending its programme.

Leeds City Council's nursery centres combine day nursery facilities with nursery education for the older pre-school children and with facilities for school-age children. One of Leeds nursery centres shares its facilities with a day centre for the elderly, facilitating inter-generational contact.

North Tyneside Council Childcare Enterprise runs a range of services co-ordinated through a 'childcare shop', where parents can go to explain their requirements and be directed to relevant services, which include childminders and nannies, nurseries, out-of-school schemes, extra care for sick children, or for children whose regular carers are sick, and a consultancy service for employers and other interested organisations. The scheme is seen as an essential component of the local authority's strategy in aiding economic development and regeneration, combating poverty and promoting equal opportunities; it was developed through corporate planning. Local employers are offered places within the scheme, and some are helped to establish new services, in partnership with the local authority.

Glasgow nursery partnership initiative. This has been launched by the Scottish Development Agency (now Scottish Enterprise) in conjunction with district and regional councils, education and training organisations and a number of small and large employers in the Glasgow area. Initiated as an EC Childcare Action Project, it was approved in the summer of 1991 by the Scottish Office and involves the provision of 160 places by day nurseries and a small number of childminders directly employed by the scheme. A further 50 places are to be added each year. The scheme will be run as a company limited by guarantee with charitable status, and funded from public and private sector sources, with some 'in kind' contributions such as premises. It is intended to help parents gain access not only to employment but also to education and training – thereby enhancing the skills of the local labour supply. Its objectives are:

(1) To demonstrate that day nurseries are beneficial in retaining and attracting parents to work, training or full-time education.

(2) To demonstrate that financial commitment to nurseries is worthwhile for industry, commerce and higher education institutions.

(3) To support the development of deprived areas by suppling subsidised childcare facilities to the long-term unemployed.

(4) To demonstrate that, after initial agency funding, partnerships of this kind are financially viable.

A particular feature of the scheme is the direct employment of childminders. The purpose of this is to provide parents of young infants with an alternative option to nursery care; to provide the possibility of caring for sick children in their own homes; to improve the links between the two forms of care (day nurseries and childminding), enhancing the quality and flexibility of care, and thereby parental choice.

Fife Regional Council is developing a Partnership in Childcare scheme. This involves the establishment of five partnership nurseries offering places to local employers. In addition to daycare for preschool children, provision includes childcare for school age children and some care for sick children. Fife receives funds for this project from the EC Regional Development Fund and from the European Social Fund.

Keighley, West Yorkshire: a local group of the lone-parent organisation, Gingerbread, set up Kiddieclub, which offers comprehensive family support to lone parents. It began as a nursery to meet what was perceived to be a desperate need for childcare in the area, and quickly grew to include before- and after-school care, and holiday provision. Priority is given to lone parents' children, but the stability of the child is put first and there are some two-parent families at the club. There is a voluntary management committee consisting of parents and community representives. The club originally received funds from the Manpower Services Commission, which ended in 1988. It is now part-funded by Bradford City Council. Fees are kept to a minimum. Two basic scales operate: one for lone parents and one for two-wage earner families; there are sliding scales for siblings.

Hammersmith and Fulham council in west London has developed the Bradmore Kids Workshop as a pilot project, combining out-of-school play facilities with a care service for children aged five to 12. It has large purpose-built premises, including a large play area outside, an indoor hall for snooker and table-tennis, a craft room and a 'quiet room'. It takes up to 65 children in term time and up to 80 in the holidays, with a staff/child ratio of about one to 10. It is open in term time from 3.30 pm until 7.00 pm (7.30 pm in the summer); places are free, except in holidays, when there is a small charge of £2 per day. Children are registered for attendance and must be collected by an authorised adult. The scheme has proved highly successful and has a long waiting list. The local authority is now planning to develop other out-of-school projects along similar lines.

Camden, north London. The Social Services Department is considering a new charging policy which centres around a core day (9.30 am to 3.30 pm) free to all parents, whether provided in Camden schools (through the Education Department) or in nursery centres or nursery groups. An income-related fee would be charged to parents for time outside the core period.

Denmark. In the rural parish of Hover, a group of parents developed an age-integrated daycare centre to meet the needs of children under ten. The centre offers pre-school and school-age children childcare in modules of 10, 20, 30, 40 and 50 hours a week. Currently, 32 children are enrolled. The parents manage the centre and employ professionally qualified staff. Sixty-five per cent of the cost is met by the municipality through grant aid (known as the 'bag of money' system). The centre is seen as strengthening the parish, the school and the life of the local community.

France. Legislation in 1981 legitimised the *creches sauvages* movement (parent-run day nurseries) which had developed from the late 1960s. The Association des Collectifs Enfants/Parents/Professionels (ACEP), was set up in the same year and is widely seen as responsible for having encouraged greater flexibility within the French structure of services. Like the UK playgroup movement, it has helped develop greater recognition of the role parents can play in collective childcare. In France this has involved a partnership between parents and professionals in providing daycare and other services. ACEP is now assisting the development of services by black and minority ethnic groups and has a growing number of rural members. It is developing provision in rural areas, as is the Federation Nationale des Associations de Familles Rurales (FNAFR). In services run by the latter organisation, parents are involved in management, but not in the provision of care. The French rural childcare programmes are seen as an important element in a wider development programme. ACEP, for example, has funding from the French Ministry of Agriculture for a pilot programme in areas designated for rural development. Addressing the needs of families with young children is seen as essential if rural areas are to retain their populations.

Employment provisions

This report has emphasised that childcare services cannot be considered without reference to employment provisions such as parental leave. These ensure that all parents, not just those who can afford it, have a measure of choice about when to care for their children themselves. A statutory framework is required to ensure adequate support (including financial support) for employed and self-employed women during pregnancy including the right to return to their existing employment following a period of maternity leave. The statutory framework should also ensure that all employed and self-employed parents, mother and fathers, have access to leave and working arrangements which support their parenting role. These proposals are explored in greater detail in a forthcoming IPPR report (Bransbury). They should include:

- Adequate provision for pregnancy and for a period of 16-20 weeks of paid maternity leave following the birth of the child for all pregnant women in employment and self employment.
- A minimum of 10 days' paid paternity leave.
- Six months' parental leave for each working parent.
- Family leave relating to the care of sick children. The number of days offered for leave could be related to the age of the child.
- Flexible working arrangements (including access to part-time parental leave.)

Funding sources

Who should pay for childcare? Three main potential sources of funds are parents, employers and government. Government contributions might include money from the EC Stuctural Funds.

Parents. There are considerable anomalies to be found in the policies of the UK and other EC countries towards parental contributions to childcare services. In general, educational services for older pre-school children are free, while parental contributions are required for daycare. This results in parents having to pay more for services for under threes. This is an issue requiring further examination; it should not detract from the principle of free nursery education but rather extend the principle to take account of developments in combining education with daycare.

In the meantime, publicly provided and funded services should not require an excessive parental contribution. The costings in this report assume an average contribution from parents of 30 per cent of the total costs of a childcare place. We do not put this forward as an ideal, but as a point of departure for policy discussion. The figure is based on patterns of parental contribution in other EC countries.

If parents are expected to contribute to costs in a childcare system which aims at equitable provision, it follows that some form of fee relief must be available to lower-income groups. The figure of 30 per cent is net of any fee relief, which means that some parents would pay more and others less, or nothing at all. (It is worth considering that in future parents' claims for fee relief should diminish, because of the effect of childcare provision on their ability to earn: as more parents go out to work, fewer will require full or partial fee relief, thereby reducing public expenditure on childcare.)

Employers. It has been argued by some (notably the Equal Opportunities Commission) that employers should contribute to the costs of childcare - either through local employer levies, or through an addition to their national insurance payments. We take the view that if employers are expected to bear some of the costs of improved employment provisions (and we think they should), then they should not also be obliged to contribute to the costs of childcare.

Employers should be encouraged to enter into dialogue with local authorities about the childcare needs of their workforce and community, to participate in partnership schemes, to make contributions 'in kind' (eg. premises) and to follow best practice in their provisions for working parents. Where employers seek planning permission from local authorities, the opportunity should be seized where possible to exact an appropriate contribution to childcare provision in the area (eg. by building a nursery as part of a new development). Employers should be obliged by law to make better provision for working parents, in the form of time off and flexible working arrangements. But they should not be subject to compulsory levies for childcare.

Government. The costings in this report (see below) involve 100 per cent of funding of educational services coming from taxation as well as 70 per cent of the funding of other services (parents paying the rest). There has been some discussion of public funds being administered through a National Childcare Development Fund (EOC 1990). It would be preferable in our view if funds were administered through the local authorities who would themselves be the most extensive providers in this area, with responsibility for reviewing and responding to local needs.

Some funding could be drawn from the European structural funds, described earlier (p.54). The possibilities for this are greatest in the following areas:

- disadvantaged areas, especially Northern Ireland, which has 'objective 1' status, where childcare services are recognised as infra-structure;

- areas of industrial decline in Scotland, Wales and the North and Midlands of England; and
- in a number of rural areas in the Highlands and Islands and Galloway in Scotland, rural Wales and Devon and Cornwall.

Little use has so far been made of these possiblilities. This partly relates to the government's lack of support for public funding of childcare for working parents and partly to its 'additonality' policy (central government claws back some of the European aid by reducing its own contribution to local authority funds). Nevertheless, the European structural funds do offer the possibility of an additional funding source which could make a significant contribution, in particular, to capital and development costs of services in more disadvantaged areas. (This has not been allowed for within our cost-benefit analysis).

A sound investment: summary of cost-benefit analysis

In the final section of this report, we set out our cost-benefit analysis which suggests that public money spent on childcare is a good investment, bringing substantial returns in the medium and long term. It estimates how much it would cost to provide childcare according to three models. The least ambitious model is based on the initial target of the EC Childcare Network (for an additional 1,656,430 places). The second model is based on current provision in Denmark (for 2,740,000 places). The most ambitious model is based on the number of mothers currently in the UK workforce (4,902,970 places).

It then calculates the savings that are likely to accrue to the Treasury as a result of providing childcare. The savings come from up to 1,800,000 additional mothers going out to work, ceasing to claim benefit, gaining skills and experience, increasing their earnings and paying taxes. Our estimates are cautious. For example, our calculations of the rates of return are based only on the benefits from increased maternal employment; they do not take into account the likely benefits of creating some 600,000 new jobs in childcare. They only take account of savings from lone parents' income support. Total savings could be higher, to include savings from unpaid housing benefit and from the impact of increased employment of women whose husbands are unemployed or receiving family credit; long-term savings due to the social impact on children growing up (p.41), and costs offset by EC funding. We do not claim our study as definitive, but offer it as a basis for discussion and as a starting point for further analysis.

In spite of these disclaimers, there is strong evidence of considerable benefit. The study shows how providing childcare not only meets social needs but also galvanises the economy – by creating jobs and by increasing the supply of labour and skills, allowing the economy to be run at a higher level. We estimate that of 1.25 million children under five currently living in poverty, up to half would be brought out of poverty if the provision of childcare enabled their mothers to work. We estimate the average net gain for households with children under five, as a result of women going out to work and earning more as they increase their skills. This ranges, after tax, National Insurance and childcare fees, from £456 per annum to £3,212 per annum, per household, depending on which model of provision is followed. We estimated the rates of return on the assumption of a phasing-in period of 13 years. (This could be faster, but it is important to allow sufficient time for the development of infrastructure, including training.) The return to the Treasury after a similar period ranges from five per cent to 51 per cent. Only the very lowest of these rates, from the least ambitious model, is below the cost of capital – and that is the rate of return to the Treasury alone. The social return, combining gains to the Treasury and to households, ranges from 24 per cent to 84 per cent. The more ambitious models yield the better returns. (See Part Two for details.)

Priorities for government

It will take time and, of course, money to develop and implement a national childcare policy. What should be the priorities for central and for local government?

Central government

Strong political direction. The success of a national childcare policy will depend on central government making its commitment clear and providing a strong lead from a cabinet-level department. Deciding where to base authority and leadership is thus a priority. The growing emphasis on improving the educational content of services suggests that overall administrative responsibility for all services should be given at a government level to the Department of Education and Science (and other relevent departments in other parts of the UK). That leaves the question of who should be responsible for co-ordinating the work of different Deparments (social services, employment, environment), setting targets and making sure that they are met. Should it be the Secretary of State for Education, or another Minister - for example, a newly-created Minister for Children or for Women? The co-ordinating Ministry should be at Cabinet level and have sufficient clout to drive policies through other Departments. Unless adequate power is invested in a new children's or women's ministry, there may be a case for giving the DES responsibility for co-ordinaton as well as for administration.

Publish objectives. The next step is to publish clear objectives, along the lines set out in this report, aiming to build upon current patterns of provision, to learn from existing models of good practice and to reach specified targets within clear time limits. Objectives should encompass not only care but also employment provisions, including paid parental and family leave. They should establish priorities for action by local government (see below); they should be accompanied by goals and timetables, and by full provision for research and assessment of outcomes.

Earmark funds. Core funding should be set aside for childcare, both for local authority services and for local authority grants to independent providers. These should be administered through local authorities; additional funds should be set aside for research and assessment.

Amend the Children Act. It should be a priority for government to amend the 1989 Children Act, in order to broaden the definition of public responsibility beyond children 'in need'. Local authorities should be given a more general duty to ensure that the childcare needs of all children and families are adequately met. This would set the stage for implementing a comprehensive childcare policy, in line with UK equal opportunities legislation, and with the laws and policies of the European Community.

Local government

Develop a co-ordinated strategy, learning from successful initiatives in the UK and elsewhere (eg. North Tyneside, Strathclyde and Manchester). As with central government, this requires a clear political direction from the authority, with one department giving strong leadership.

Audit childcare needs and provision. Local authorities should begin by finding out what local people (children, parents and employers) need in the way of childcare, as well as the implications for childcare policy of local development plans. They should also conduct a thorough review of current childcare provision – their own, as well as services provided by others, exploring ways of making effective use of existing resources, and within a framework which promotes an integrated approach to the delivery of services.

Open dialogue with local employers, colleges, community-based organisations. This is a useful way of discovering local needs and maximising local resources. The dialogue should cover not only services but also ways of making the workplace and educational facilities more responsive to the needs of workers and students with children.

Publish objectives, in line with national policy, and taking account of local needs and conditions. As with central government's objectives, these should include goals and timetables, and plans for monitoring and assessing local provision as it develops.

Pursue partnership arrangements. Develop, where possible, new childcare schemes in partnership with local employers, colleges and voluntary organisations.

Develop funding strategies. Investigate (where appropriate) the possibility of EC funding. Establish procedures (if they do not already exist) for giving grants to local groups and voluntary organisations, in such a way as to encourage communities to set up childcare arrangements which suit their own needs and preferences.

Set standards and measure performance to ensure that publicly provided and publicly funded childcare services are consistent with national and local objectives.

CHILDCARE COSTS AND BENEFITS

This study examines the cost implications of the major developments in childcare provision proposed in the main body of the report and identifies potential savings and benefits from such developments. It discusses the costs and benefits of three possible programmes of public childcare for the UK which take account of the proposals outlined in the report. One is based on public childcare provision in Denmark, one is based on provision scaled to the numbers of children with mothers currently in employment or unemployed but wanting work, and the third is based on the initial minimum target of the European Community Childcare Network. Each programme uses the components for a basic structure of childcare recommended in the report (but not including informal services such as parent and toddler groups). Those considered are employment provision (parental leave); day nurseries and supported family daycare; education (nursery classes) for three and four year olds; pre-school extended hours schemes; and primary school-age after school centres.

The study involves a number of assumptions in relation to both costs and benefits. The most important of these relate to the effect of public childcare provision on maternal employment. In a version applied to all three models it is assumed that mothers with children in full-time childcare will want to work full-time and mothers with children in part-time childcare will want to work part-time. The assumption is based on the strength of demand both for public childcare and for maternal employment in countries where public childcare is available. Existing working mothers are assumed to transfer into the public childcare programme. Two variants are also presented for Model A (that based on provision in Denmark) - one assuming Danish labour force participation and one using intentions on labour force participation expressed in a Strathclyde survey.

No allowance has been made for the proposed childcare fees deflecting some of the demand - the fee subsidies to prevent demand deflection have not been examined.

Our assumptions in relation to take up of parental leave follow Holtermann (see bibliography).

We have been cautious over adding the benefits of both increased maternal employment and childcare employment. Public childcare increases both the labour supply and the demand for labour. The supply side effect can prevent the bottlenecks which make the economy inflation prone. As a result the economy might be expanded more, not only providing mothers who now join the labour force with work but also to employ some of the existing unemployed. If this happens it is possible to add together the maternal and childcare employment (even though they may be the same people). But we present our results without adding.

The first part of the study concerns the costs of the childcare programmes, both current costs and setting-up (training and capital) costs. The study then examines the likely effects of the childcare programmes on mothers' wishes for employment. Between the three programmes five versions of mothers' labour force participation are explored. We estimate the effects of increased employment in each case on tax revenues and benefit costs for government and on disposable incomes for households. We also estimate employment effects in terms of jobs in childcare.

It depends on the macro-economic situation whether extra workers (the supply side effect) or extra jobs (the demand side effect), or both, are relevent to the net costs of a childcare programme to the Exchequer, but we would argue that the effect on women's labour force participation is always relevant.

Finally, benefits in terms of poverty reduction among children, developmental benefits for children, and improvements in pay and opportunities for women are discussed and where possible quantified. Results are presented separately for government and for households in the concluding section, with rate of return calculations on financial and social bases.

Table 1: Demographic figures used for UK, years 1990 or 1991

Child population	
under 3	2,415,000
3-4	1,535,000
under 5	3,949,000
5-11	5,103,000
Population of mothers by age of youngest child	
under 5	3,074,000*
5-10	2,112,000*

*adjusted from GB figures, 2,967,000 and 2,039,000 respectively

Sources: OPCS, 1989; Department of Employment, December 1990

Table 2: Current (1988) UK childcare provision

	no. of places
public	
LA day nurseries	34,225
LEA nursery schools and classes	359,310
LEA primary school (under 5s)	297,082
non-public	
private and voluntary day nurseries	40,378*
registered childminders	189,054
playgroups	490,515

*private nursery provision is increasing rapidly, eg in 1989 there were 24% more registered places than in 1988 in England.

Source: Cohen, 1990

Targets for childcare provision

Three programmes of public childcare are explored.

Model A: Danish Model

This involves an estimate of required provision based on adopting current public provision in Denmark. In terms of mothers' employment this model supports high employment rates at part-time or full-time level.

Up to one year:	three months' parental leave (assumed take up: 20-30 per cent of under ones).
Up to three:	19.2 per cent day nursery; 28.5 per cent public family daycare; total 47.7 per cent.
Three to five:	16.4 per cent pre-school and school-age centres,10.1 per cent public familydaycare; 48.8 per cent kindergarten; total 75.2 per cent (for UK, 'kindergarten' means education/nursery class; 'pre-school and school-age centres' means day-nursery).
Six to 11:	14 per cent after-school centres; 8 per cent pre-school and school-age centres; total 22 per cent.

(*Note*: In Denmark, compulsory schooling starts at seven. The above treats six year olds as in school - the majority are in pre-primary schooling. As a source of targets for the UK the Danish three-to-five figures are applied to three-to-four year olds.)

Model B: UK Workforce Model

Provision based on current rates of mothers in the labour force in UK (plus education for 90 per cent of three and four year olds). This model enables all mothers who currently are in the labour force, including unemployed, to work full time (via outside school hours provision for all) - apart from some mothers of under threes.

Up to one:	parental leave: (three months) 20-30 per cent; (six months) 27-37 per cent.
Up to three:	provision for 38 per cent of children.

Three to four: 90 per cent in education; 40 per cent in care outside school hours.

Five to nine: outside school hours care based on 52.5 per cent of mothers in the labour force.

Model C: EC Childcare Network

Provision based on EC Childcare Network initial target. This is meant as a target 'for minimum levels of provision that all member states should meet as quickly as possible, and at most during the next 5 years' (Moss,1988, 265). The model provides more limited support for full-time employment of mothers, and for any employment whilst children are under three, than in the other two models.

Up to one: parental leave.

Up to three: places for 10 per cent of children (full-time equivalent).

Three to four: 70 per cent in education, plus 15 per cent in care outside school hours.

Five to 11: 15 per cent in care outside school hours.

Table 3: Numbers for models A, B and C

<1	parental leave:	156,000 – 229,000 (3 months) 210,000 – 283,000 (6 months)

3 months is assumed for the Danish model (Danish parental leave is actually 10 weeks) and 3 and 6 months as options for the other 2 models. The figures are calculated from Holtermann (see below).

<3 each of these is calculated on the basis of a quarter of places part-time

Model A:	1,007,960 full-time equivalent places mix: day nurseries 405,720, public fam. daycare 602,240
Model B:	802,990 full-time equivalent places mix: day nurseries 535,300, public fam. daycare 267,700
Model C:	241,500 full-time equivalent places mix: day nurseries 161,000, public fam. daycare 80,500

3-4	Model A:	education 749,570, day nurseries 251,900 public family daycare 155,140
	Model B:	education 1,382,400 outside school hours care 614,400
	Model C:	education 1,075,200 outside school hours care 230,400

5-11 outside school hours care

Model A:	1,122,660
Model B:	2,679,080
Model C:	765,450

Table 4: Totals of children with places in the 3 models

(not including parental leave)

Model A	3,430,600
Model B	4,979,180
Model C	2,116,650

NB: child, 3-4, with place at both nursery school and outside school hours centre is counted only once.

Current costs of childcare

Parental leave

The cost of parental leave is estimated using Holtermann, including her assumptions about take-up. But we have used 1990/1 figures rather than 1985 which means more eligible parents, because of higher annual births (770,000), and higher economic activity rates among mothers of second and third children. This gives the annual numbers interested in a three month parental leave entitlement, including fathers, as 156,000 to 229,000, and the numbers who would take-up a six month parental leave as 210,000 to 283,000. Holtermann estimates the cost of such a scheme assuming a flat-rate benefit equal to the statutory sick pay rate. At 1990 rates that would be £39.25 per week. For three months that would cost £510.25 per person, or from £79.6m to £116.8m per year in aggregate. For six months it would cost £1,020.50 per person, or £214.2m to £288.7m per year. These are gross costs, before allowance for savings.

Day nurseries

The average cost per filled place in 1989-90 is given as £5,471 in CIPFA (1991). The England and Wales total net expenditure (which deducts parental contributions) is estimated at £110.83m, equal to approximately £129.9m for UK. Gross expenditure is estimated at £135m. Although there are some 34,225 places, occupancy is given as 74 per cent.

Nursery schooling

The cost of a nursery class place in 1986/7 is given as £975 per annum in the DES Memorandum to House of Commons Select Committee (1988-9). The equivalent at 1989/90 prices is £1,304, inflating at the increase in cost per full time equivalent (FTE) for under fives in *The Government's Expenditure Plans,1990/1-92/3*, Cm.1014, 1991. The total UK cost is estimated at £628.67m in 1988/9 (the date of the pupil numbers quoted above) and £691.76m in 1989/90.

Public family daycare

This is not currently available in the UK which makes it difficult to cost. Cohen (1988) reports charges by registered childminders of £27 to £35 per week in 1986, which would be approximately £38 to £50 in 1990. But this low cost relative to day nurseries is largely because provision is not supported. Moss (1988 p.88) points out that the ratio in France is 66 to 80 per cent. In Denmark it is 58 per cent in general and 69 per cent in bigger towns. Using 58 per cent in relation to the cost of day nurseries in Britain gives a cost of £3,184 per year or £64 a week per child place (1989/90).

After-school centres

Simpson (1986) quotes 'topping and tailing' costs for three and four year olds at £42 per week (1984). But after-school and holiday care for five to 11 year olds is estimated at £400 per child per year (1984). A more recent estimate for after-school and holiday provision is £29 to £36 per week, or £1,508 to £1,879 per year (Kids Clubs Network, 1990). We propose to use £2,640 per annum (£55 per week) for the higher costs for three and four year olds and £1,690 per annum for after-school and holiday provision for five to 11 year olds.

Funding Assumptions

Parental leave is assumed to be funded by National Insurance, nursery education is assumed to be funded by central taxation in full, but current costs of other provision is assumed to be shared in the following proportions:

Central/local government	70 per cent
Parents	30 per cent

This ratio leads to childcare fees for parents as set out in Table 5. It is assumed that some fee relief is provided so that the fees are affordable for all parents.

Table 5: Average parental contributions, meeting 30% of costs

day nurseries	£1641 pa or £34 pw
supported family daycare	£955 pa or £20 pw
after-school centre, 3-4 year old	£792 pa or £16 pw
after school centre, 5-11 year old	£507 pa or £10 pw

In Tables 6, 7 and 8, total gross current costs per year are set out for the three programmes. Then in Table 9 the difference in costs between present public provision and the three total programme costs are presented.

Table 6: Cost of Model A

parental leave		£79.6m–£116.8m
<3	day nurseries	£2219.7m
	public family daycare	£1917.5m
3-4	education	£977.4m
	day nurseries	£1378.1m
	public family daycare	£494.0m
5-11	outside school hours care	£1897.3m
Total		£8963.6m–£9000.8m

Table 7: Cost of Model B

parental leave	3 mth.	£79.6m–£116.8m
	6 mth.	£214.2m–£288.7m
<3	day nurseries	£2928.6m
	public fam. daycare	£852.4m
3-4	education	£1802.6m
	outside school hours care	£1622.0m
5-11	outside school hours care	£4527.6m
total (with 3 mth. parental leave)		£11812.8m
total (with 6 mth. parental leave)		£11947.4m

Table 8: Cost of Model C

parental leave	3 mth.	£79.6m–£116.8m
	6 mth.	£214.2m–£288.7m
<3	day nurseries	£880.8m
	public fam. daycare	£256.3m
3-4	education	£1402.1m
	outside school hours care	£608.3m
5-11	outside school hours care	£1293.6m
total (with 3 mth. parental leave)		£4520.7m
total (with 6 mth. parental leave)		£4655.5m

Table 9: Extra costs of the costed targets over 1989/90 public provision in the UK

a. Current provision costs

day nurseries	£135.0m
education for <5s	£691.8m
total	£826.8m

b. Extra costs for

Model A	£8,136.8m
Model B	£10,986.0m*
Model C	£3,693.9m*

*based on first versions above

c. Funding for extra new provision in £ million

	government	nat. insurance	parents
Model A	5,690.3	79.6	2,366.9
Model B	7,932.3	79.6	2,974.1
Model C	2,707.7	79.6	906.6

Employment in childcare

The major component of costs of childcare is staffing. We present here our estimates of the numbers of staff required for the three programmes taking account of new guidelines in relation to day nurseries and allowing for improvements envisaged for nursery education by the Rumbold Report.

Table 10: Staff members in the target programmes

<3 Model A: (1,007,960 full-time equivalent places)
day nurseries 110,843, public family daycare 200,747

Model B: (802,990 full-time equivalent places)
day nurseries 146,245, public family daycare 89,233

Model C: (241,500 full-time equivalent places)
day nurseries 43,985, public family daycare 26,800

3-4 Model A: (1,156,610 places)
education 74,957, day nurseries 50,380
public family daycare 51,713
Model B: (1,996,800 places)
education 138,240, outside school hours care 122,880

Model C: (1,305,600 places)
education 107,520, outside school hours care 46,080

5-11 outside school hours care

Model A: (1,122,660 places) 74,844

Model B: (2,679,080 places) 178,605

Model C: (765,450 places) 51,030

Table 11: Totals of staffing in 3 models

Model	Staff
Model A	563,484
Model B	675,203
Model C	275,415

Current staff in public childcare is estimated as follows: **Day nurseries**: 12,622 full-time equivalent staff is estimated from CIPFA, 1991 (grossing up for UK). **Education of under 5s**: pupil/staff ratios were 8.5 in nursery schools and 10.7 in nursery classes in 1987 (DES evidence to House of Commons Select Committee, 1988-9). Under 5s in primary classes are hard similarly to quantify. Applying these rates to child numbers gives some 35,265 staff in nursery schools and classes, and using 1:12 as the ratio for primary classes gives 24,757 staff for under 5s in primary classes. Total current staffing in education of under 5s is therefore estimated at 60,022. Around half of these will be teachers, and half nursery assistants.

Table 12: Extra staffing to meet the models we have costed

Model A	490,840
Model B	602,559
Model C	202,771

Training and capital costs

We use table 12 (with 10) above to derive numbers of trained staff required (see table 13). These figures cannot be exact, eg many trained nursery nurses are employed in the private childcare sector and might transfer to the public sector. But the size of numbers required points to a need for phasing in for any of the programmes. The scale of training at present is well below requirements The number of nursery nurses in training in 1987 was 12,245 (House of Commons Select Committee, 1988/9). Teachers newly qualifying for nursery/primary level in 1989 numbered 6,712 in England (approx. 8,000 in UK).

Table 13: Numbers of new trained staff required

	Model A	Model B	Model C
teachers	7,470	39,110	23,750
nursery nurses	282,300	217,350	68,510
out school carers	37,400	150,740	48,560

Assumptions: half of public family daycare providers are trained nursery nurses; half are untrained (or from existing childminders); half of outside school hours care providers are trained, half not.

We now consider the cost of the required training. The tuition costs for teachers in training in 1988/9 is given as £197m, and the teachers enrolled in training 34,300 (both figures exclude University Depts of Education, who had a further 8,300). This means the cost per place per year is £5,743, or £23,000 for a four year course. (Figures from DES,1990 and Central Statistical Office,1991.) Using that figure, and a 'guesstimate' for the training costs of nursery nurses and outside school hours carers of £9,000 for a two-year course, we can estimate training costs for the new staff as in Table 14. These figures do not include student grants (only applicable to teachers).

Table 14: Training costs

	in £ million		
	Model A	Model B	Model C
teachers	172	900	546
nursery nurses	2,541	1,956	617
out school carers	337	1,357	437
Total	3,050	4,213	1,600

It should be noted that Table 14 refers to newly required staff. By way of comparison the total cost of training for the three programmes, were they starting from scratch, would be: Model A £4,124m, Model B £5,287m, and Model C £2,674m (assuming the same unit costs).

Capital costs are very difficult to estimate. In many areas conversion of existing premises will be possible rather than requiring new buildings. Some cost per place figures:

Day nurseries: we have averaged figures from Glasgow and the London Borough of Camden, mainly involving conversions, to produce an approximate figure of £2,500 per place. No allowance is made for take over of existing non-public provision, although in places that might be a source of saving.

Nursery classes: the House of Commons Select Committee (1988-9) quote Stockport LEA evidence of capital cost per place of £3,000 for a nursery class in a new unit, £750 for a nursery class in adapted existing school, and £3,750 for a new nursery school. The 1990 equivalents are approximately £860, £3,450, and £4,300. If we make the assumption of provision being an average of the first two types the cost per place is £2,155.

Supported family daycare: equipment costs of £80 per place notional estimate. Although many existing childminders would come into a public scheme we assume all have a one-off equipment allowance (further small-scale equipment would be in running cost).

After-school hours: We estimate equipment costs at £156 per place, based on Kids Clubs Network estimate of £97m needed to equip the clubs they envisage (Equal Opportunities Commission, 1990).

Table 15: Capital costs

	in £ million		
	Model A	Model B	Model C
day nurseries	1,558.5	1,252.7	316.9
family daycare	60.6	21.4	6.4
education	200.8	1,564.5	902.5
after school	175.1	453.9	155.4
Total	1,995.0	3,292.5	1,381.2

Income generated by employment of mothers

This is a crucial aspect of the benefits of childcare. It leads to a better standard of living and less poverty for many households, and fewer benefit outlays and more revenue for government. However it is very difficult to estimate. Employment has been rising rapidly amongst mothers of under-five and school age children without increases in publicly supported childcare (apart from rising places in education for three and four year olds). We have to recognise that a programme of public childcare will partly go to families whose mothers already work and who will switch from private or informal childcare to the public childcare. This is what is known as the 'deadweight' effect of public provision (cf. Metcalf and Leighton).

But we know that many parents (in particular mothers) are prevented from taking paid work (or work shorter hours than they would wish) because of childcare responsibilities. The evidence includes:

- The much lower labour force participation of mothers of under fives compared with women in general.
- The higher labour force participation of mothers of under fives in countries with more extensive public childcare (the example of Denmark will be used here).

- In surveys a high proportion of mothers of under fives say they would like to take paid work if affordable childcare were available. One such survey is that in Strathclyde Region by Scott (1989): she found that 73 per cent of mothers of children under five wanted to work. This is very similar to the current numbers in Denmark, although the Strathclyde preferences were for 20 per cent full-time and 54 per cent part-time work, whereas among Danish mothers 45 per cent work full-time and 28 per cent part-time.

The number of mothers of children under 11 who are in employment but who do not have public childcare is at least 1,540,000. Deadweight is therefore potentially high, given the number of new childcare places in our three models (2,740,000, 4,902,970, and 1,656,600 respectively). But most of the current employment is part-time, so that there is much scope for the hours of part-time workers to be lengthened, should they want this.

It is sometimes argued that the rise in the labour force induced by childcare will not necessarily be matched by jobs (Simpson). Particularly in a period of high unemployment jobs won by the new members of the labour force might just be at the expense of jobs for others. However it is widely recognised that the British economy suffers from supply constraints as well as, at times, demand deficiency. Whenever the economy booms these supply constraints create inflationary pressures and the boom has to be curtailed. The extra labour force, much of it skilled, will relax the supply constraints, so demand can be kept up when it would not otherwise be deemed safe. In addition, in the longer term, the number of jobs does keep pace with labour supply expansion. We will later look at job creation in childcare itself as a result of the programmes here. That is a source of income generation in areas of demand constraint, as the labour supply effect is in areas of supply constraint.

Employment of mothers in relation to target provision

Model A

Version One. The basis for employment changes presented here is that the work rate of UK mothers of children aged up to four and five to 11 would change to that of Danish mothers of similar aged children if UK public childcare were as in Denmark. This clearly involves the strong assumption that all the participation difference between the two countries is due to the childcare difference. The resulting labour supply expansion is 1,709,900 more full time and 79,000 more part time.

Table 16: UK and Danish employment participation rates compared

	<5 UK	Denmark	5-9 UK	Denmark
full-time	11.3	45.9	13.9	44.5
part-time	25.3	28.9	38.7	37.2
total	36.5	74.8	52.5	81.6

Version Two. A further variant is to use the Strathclyde survey. This produced similar totals of desired work for mothers of under fives as in Denmark now but it maintained the existing British bias to part time work. With changes from present British employment rates for mothers of under fives to the preferences expressed in that survey we get 267,440 more full-time workers and 882,240 more part-time workers. For mothers of school age children, who were not covered in the survey, we assume the same employment rate as in Denmark, but divide it 50:50 between full-time and part-time. This produces an overall expansion, including the mothers of under fives, of 574,400 full-time and 1,189,240 part-time.

Version Three. Both versions above involve a very strong response of labour force participation to the extra childcare provision. But Danish mothers' labour force participation may not be created here by Danish levels of public childcare because of other influences affecting employment rates. We have therefore used another approach - also attempted with the other models for comparison. We begin by noting that for under fives Model A provides for 1,271,000 full-time childcare places and 1,037,600 part-time places (the division between full and part-time is not exact). The population of mothers of under fives is 78 per cent of the population of children under five because of families with two or more children. Applying that percentage to the proposed numbers of places gives 991,400 mothers (32 per cent) able to work full-time and 809,300 (26 per cent) able to work part-time. The outside school hours provision for five to 11 year olds allows 22 per cent of mothers with youngest child in that age group to work full-time (464,600). Mothers with children both under and over 5 are assumed to be able to get childcare for all their children if they wish to work full-time. We shall assume that the numbers with children aged five to 11 working part-time remain unchanged (38.7 per cent, or 817,300). This approach involves much more 'deadweight', i.e. we are assuming the existing employed mothers absorb much of the new childcare. Alternatively one can say that the other versions imply more continuing informal childcare arrangements.

Model B

This involves the largest expansion of childcare places of our three models, some 4,902,970. It however involves fewer places for under threes than the Model A, more education places for over threes, and many more after school care places. Although called a workforce model, it involves more than providing a childcare place for all children whose mothers are in the workforce - particularly as education is provided for 90 per cent of three to four year olds. The study by Townson of Canada has a workforce model with no labour force expansion implied - an extreme 'deadweight' assumption. We believe that it is more realistic to have a labour supply effect, and in this case, with large-scale after school provision, particularly towards full-time work.

Following the approach in Version Three of Model A above, we have derived an estimate of the employment impact as follows:

- for under fives the model provides 1,302,400 full-time places and 997,700 part-time places (including as part-time, education places not matched by an after-school hours place). Applying a 78 per cent ratio of working mothers to children for this age group gives 1,015,900 mothers (33 per cent) able to work full-time and 778,200 (25.3 per cent) able to work part-time.

- The extensive outside school hours provision for five to 11 year olds allows 52.5 per cent of mothers with youngest child in that age group to work full-time (1,108,800). Allowing for some mothers of children five to 11 being out of the labour force, we shall assume that 30 per cent (633,600) work part-time. Overall labour force participation for this group of mothers is then marginally higher than in Denmark, appropriate for greater childcare.

Model C

We do not propose to use exactly the approach adopted for Model B because that would mean virtually no effect on employment even though 1,656,600 new public childcare places would be provided. Instead we limit the deadweight as follows. The Model provides 1,202,850 full-time places which implies 657,970 mothers wanting to work full-time. We assume a third of these places are taken by existing full-time workers, which means 438,650 existing full-time workers remain in work but do not transfer to public childcare. This leads to an increase of 455,690 full-time workers. The demand for part-time work comes to 712,760 for mothers of under-fives, a fall of 64,940, and is assumed to be equal to present numbers, minus transfers into full-time work for mothers of 5-11 year olds, a fall of 234,430. The full range of options is explored in Table 17. The proportions of employed mothers of under-11s who work full-time range between 60 per cent for Model B, 46 per cent for Model C and 30 per cent for Model A2 (the current figure for the UK is 29 per cent).

Table 17: Present and increase in number of mothers working

	under 5		5-11	
	full-time	part-time	full-time	part-time
Present	347,360	777,700	293,570	817,350
Model A				
version 1	+1,063.600	+110,700	+646,300	–31,700
version 2	+267,440	+882,240	+307,000	+307,000
version 3	+644,040	+31,600	+171,000	0
Model B	+668,540	0	+815,200	-183,400
Model C	+221,260	–64,960	+234,430	–234,430

We illustrate the variety of effects schematically in Table 18. It should be noted that in the three versions constructed along the same lines (A3, B, C), A3 and B have proportionately more effect on employment than C because the 'deadweight' effect is smaller in the bigger programmes.

Table 18: Ratios – employment increase to increase in public childcare places

	version	ratio
Model A	1	65%
	2	65%
	3	31%
Model B		30%
Model C		11%

Income generated by the new employment

We need next to estimate the earnings from the extra employment postulated. For mothers of under fives we propose to use the average earnings rate for 25-29 year old women here, which according to the New Earnings Survey in 1990 was £11,227 per annum for full-time workers and £3,858 per annum for part-time workers. For mothers of school-age children we use the earnings rates for 30-39 year old women (£11,934 and £4,056 respectively). We shall later present some calculations for the impact on wages of the greater experience that women will be able to bring to the labour market as a result of having less time out of the labour force for childcare. We are assuming that the extra labour supply does not reduce earnings.

The next table illustrates the extra gross earnings for our different models of the employment generation of childcare expansion.

Table 19: Extra gross earnings from mothers' increased labour force participation

in £ million

	under 5		5-11	
	full-time	part-time	full-time	part-time
Model A				
version 1	11,941.0	427.1	7,712.9	–128.6
version 2	3,002.1	3,403.7	3,663.7	1,245.2
version 3	7,230.6	121.9	2,040.7	0
Model B	7,505.7	0	9,728.6	–743.9
Model C	2,484.1	–250.6	2,797.7	–950.8

In total the extra earnings are as in Table 20:

Table 20: Totals for extra earnings

		in £ million
1. Model A	1	19,952.4
	2	11,314.7
	3	9,393.3
2. Model B		16,490.4
3. Model C		4,080.4

Government revenues from extra employment

On an average extra full-time worker earning £11,227 per annum.

Income tax:	with married women's allowance of £2,605 and tax rate of 25 per cent: £2,155.50
National insurance (employee and employer):	average employee pays £789.88 (assuming 30 per cent contract out); employer pays £1,072.57 for such an employee.
Indirect tax:	assuming average disposable income of £8,282 and 22 per cent average tax rate (UK National Accounts, tables 4.1 and 9.5): £1,822.

Total flow back to Exchequer, £5,840 (52.02 per cent of earnings).

With similar calculations for the mothers with youngest children of primary school age and for part-timers, the aggregate flow back from our various models of employment is as follows:

Table 21: Tax flowback from extra employment of mothers

		in £ million
1. Model A	1	10,357.6
	2	5,203.5
	3	4,874.1
2. Model B		8,716.5
3. Model C		2,307.0

Benefit savings from employment of mothers

Taking single parents off Income Support. This exercise is based on figures for lone parents of children under five. We start with the following data:

- Lone mothers with youngest child under five: 462,000 (Dept. of Employment,1990).
- UK and Danish employment rates of lone mothers with a child up to four (figures are percentages):

	UK	Denmark
full-time	6.3	38.9
part-time	11.7	30.7
Total	18.1	69.5

(Cohen,1990)

That lone mothers would like to work to an extent similar to Denmark is indicated by the finding in a recent survey of lone mothers that 65 per cent of those with children under 5 would like to work if childcare were available (Bradshaw and Millar). There is even a willingness among many to work part-time in spite of the financial disincentive posed by losing Income Support pound-for-pound.

To move from present British employment of single parents to the Danish rate involves increasing full-timers by 32.6 per cent and part-timers by 19 per cent. The saving for full-timers would be £53.25 a week (assuming April 1990 rates, one child per household, child benefit £7.25) but less for part-timers, 86 per cent of whom still receive some Income Support - say £35 a week saving.

£53.25 x 52 x (32.6% x 462,000) = £2,769 p.a. x 150,612 = £417.04m.
£35 x 52 x (19% x 462,000) = £1,820 p.a. x 87,780 = £159.76m.

We have made various assumptions for the other cases

:

Table 22: Benefit savings for lone parents

			in £ million
1. Model A	1	(ft+32.6%; pt +19%)	576.8
	2	(ft+11%; pt + 40%)	477.0
	3	(ft+22%; pt + 10%)	365.5
2. Model B		(ft+22%; pt + 10%)	365.5
3. Model C		(ft+9%; pt + 7%)	174.0

Taking family with unemployed man off Income Support. This involves the same disincentive to working part-time noted in the single parent case. As a result (and extending to full-time work too) there is a widespread reluctance for wives to go out to work when their husbands are unemployed. In view of this the savings in Income Support for this group would be particularly speculative to predict and will not be pursued.

Housing Benefit saving. This is a saving of government expenditure from the rise in income of all rented households as a result of the mother working (or increasing work hours) because of the availability of childcare. But the calculation is very difficult and will not be pursued here.

Disposable income effect

In Table 23, we can get an idea of the impact of these programmes on household disposable income by taking the extra earnings figures from Table 20 and subtracting benefits lost (from table 22) and income tax, employee National Insurance, indirect taxes and the childcare fees (from table 9). The average gain for households with children under 11, can be obtained by dividing any of the numbers in the table by 5.2 as there are approximately 5,200,000 such households. The average gain however conceals wide variations - many households would not increase their incomes at all.

Table 23: Boost to disposable income from extra employment of mothers

in £ million		Increase in household income after:		
		income tax and NI	income tax NI & indirect tax	income tax, NI indirect tax & childcare fee
Model A	1	14,149.7	11,204.4	8,837.5
	2	8,472.0	6,682.2	4,315.3
	3	6,649.0	5,186.0	2,819.0
Model B		11,822.0	9,221.0	6,247.0
Model C		2,612.9	2,055.5	1,148.9

Poverty Impact

We have already noted that child poverty is correlated with mothers not working (p.35). This means that, if public childcare can be made available for these children, there is scope for a significant reduction in child poverty. DSS (1990) reports that 3,090,000 children were in households with below 50 per cent of average income in 1987, a commonly used poverty measure (see Oppenheim,1990): that is 26 per cent of all children. 1,180,000 (38 per cent) of these had heads of household in full-time work, 730,000 (25 per cent) were headed by lone parents not in full-time work, and 960,000 (31 per cent) were in households where the head was unemployed. We have attempted to estimate how many under fives are in poverty by using the Family Expenditure Survey (Central Statistical Office,1987 table 7). In households with net disposable income under £150 a week there are 27.2 per cent of all children and 33 per cent of children under five. Although the poverty threshold, 50 per cent of average income, is different for different household sizes (equivalence scales are applied to incomes), we should not be far wrong in inferring that 31.5 per cent of under fives are in poverty by this definition, based on maintaining the same differential over the 26 per cent of all children who are in that position. This means 1,126,800 in Great Britain, or some 1,244,000 in the UK.

It is clear that the vast majority of the mothers of these under fives in poverty are not working. Even in terms of all children in poverty that is true (cf. Central Statistical Office 1987 table 26). It is likely that a high proportion of these would be brought out of poverty if the mother could work as a result of available childcare. The average contribution of the wife to the gross income of households with a working wife and dependent children was £91 a week (Central Statistical Office 1987, table 21).

However single parents and unemployed families have least to gain financially because of their loss of Income Support. Many of these might choose not to work and the children would remain in poverty. We do not know the proportions of children under five in poverty who are in households with an unemployed father or no father. We can only assume that these are the same as for all children in households with less than 50 per cent of average income. That is 56 per cent of the children in poverty. So some 697,000 of the 1,244,000 under 5 children in poverty have mothers with reduced incentive to respond to public childcare by going out to work. But we would still expect many to do so, as the earlier analysis on taking single parents off Income Support suggests. The reduced incentive applies mainly to working part-time, for full-time work would normally more than compensate for the loss of Income Support and can be supplemented with Family Credit (if known about) for low paid jobs. Family Credit itself may act as a disincentive for a spouse to work where there is one earner in the household. Overall, however, we expect that up to half of the under fives in poverty could be brought out of poverty by the kind of public childcare programmes analysed here.

The poverty figures quoted are for 1987; they are very sensitive to the numbers of unemployed and may well be lower in 1990 because of the unemployment decrease between the two years.

Exchequer flowback from jobs created in childcare

It depends on the macro-economic situation whether the jobs created in childcare add to jobs overall. If the economy is 'supply constrained' then extra demand in one direction (eg childcare) has to be matched by reduced demand elsewhere. But a powerful feature of childcare provision is that it increases the supply of workers as well as creating a demand itself. That means we can potentially consider gains in terms of incomes and a tax flowback to the Exchequer from the jobs created in childcare as well as the incomes and tax flowback from the increased labour supply. Where there is unemployment there is potentially both new income creation (with tax flowbacks) and benefit savings.

Salary assumptions

Flowback figures are particularly relevent for short-run demand-deficiency situations so that we are looking for salary levels close to starting salaries.

Nursery nurses: Cohen (1988) reports average starting salaries 77 per cent of the average for non-manual women as a whole. This would give a figure of £8,700 for 1990. But we want to allow for some improvement in these rates so we have used £9,500 in the calculations below.

Day nurseries have other staff as well as nursery nurses. In the absence of evidence we shall not pursue the flowback from their employment.

Supported family daycare staff: Childminder pay rates are generally very low. Public provision of the service will have to involve an improvement. Good schemes now use NJC scale pay rates of £6,957-£8,364 (points 6-14, 1990 rates). We shall take the average, £7,660. Eventually these staff would need to be qualified nursery nurses and pay here would be similar to day nurseries, but then our costings would have to be revised upwards. Moss reports that internationally pay is lower for these staff than nursery staff (Moss,1988).

Nursery teachers: The average earnings of nursery and primary teachers (female) according to the New Earnings Survey (Dept. of Employment,1990) is £14,872. Starting salaries are around £11,500 (inferred from DES,1986 where salaries of teachers under 25 are about 77 per cent of the average). We propose to use £12,300. We shall assume that half the staffing of nursery classes is teachers and half is nursery assistants (with nursery nurse qualifications and salaries).

After-school centres: Again staffing will involve an officer-in-charge and trained assistants. We shall pursue flowback calculations only in relation to the latter, and assume their salaries are the same as nursery nurses, £9,500.

Table 24 uses these salaries to estimate the extra incomes to childcare workers in our three models. These figures use the staffing figures in Table 12 and are consistent with the cost figures in Table 9.

Table 24: Incomes in extra childcare employment

		in £ million	
	Model A	Model B	Model C
day nurseries	1411.7	1269.4	297.9
family daycare	1933.8	683.5	205.3
education	162.7	852.5	517.7
out-school hours	711.0	2864.1	922.5
total	4219.2	5669.5	1943.4

From these figures of income generated we can calculate flowbacks to the Exchequer via Income Tax, National Insurance contributions, indirect taxes.

Table 25: Exchequer 'flowbacks' from individual childcare employees

		Annual amounts in £s	
pay	7660	9500	12300
tax	1264	1724	2424
employee NI	417	545	741
employer NI	489	723	874
indirect tax	1153	1432	1809
total	3323	4424	5848

Assumptions: as in government revenues from extra employment, p.112, but all treated as contracted out of full NI, with allowance for private pension contribution in expenditure/indirect tax.

Benefit saving would be £1,942 per year (Unemployment Benefit £37.35 per week) for those recruited directly or indirectly from the unemployment register. It is difficult to tell the proportion of hiring which reduces the unemployment register. Particularly in the case of women many come from unregistered unemployment where they have no benefit. We shall adopt an assumption that for every job filled by women from the registered unemployed there are three filled by women off the register. This would mean that for one in four of the new childcare employees the flowback will be £1,942 plus £3,323/4,424/ 5,848 according to salary.

Table 26: Total flowbacks from childcare employment

in £ million

	taxes	benefits	Total
Model A	1,904.1	238.3	2,142.4
Model B	2,623.1	292.6	2,915.7
Model C	901.4	98.5	1,000.0

Replacement of staff on parental leave

We have already estimated the take-up of parental leave (at three months' leave 156,000 to 229,000; six months' leave 210,000 to 283,000).

Only a certain proportion of these will be replaced and only some will be new jobs - those where it is not the case that the parent resigns and would have done so anyway without the leave. We shall use Holtermann's estimate that a quarter of the leaves involve replacements which would not have happened anyway. We also again need an assumption as to what proportion of the new jobs involve recruitment from the unemployment register. Because a portion will be men we shall assume more are from the register than in the case of childcare staff. We shall assume here that a half of recruits are from the register. The resulting estimated benefit savings are:

3 months' leave: £9.5m to £13.9m.
6 months' leave: £25.5m to £34.4m.

The tax flowbacks are the taxing of the parental leave allowance and the taxing of the temporary replacement jobs. Our estimate for taxing the leave allowance (for the three-quarters currently assumed to resign their job - half of whom are assumed to pay the basic rate on it) is:

3 months' leave £7.5m to £11.0m.
6 months' leave £20.1m to £27.1m.

The estimated tax and NI for the temporary jobs (assuming 50 per cent remain below the tax threshold with 3 month jobs) is:

3 months' leave £69.9m to £102.6m.
6 months' leave £212.4m to £285.2m.

These are much higher figures than Holtermann's. We are applying the flowbacks to all the replacements of leave-takers who return and we include indirect taxes (as with childcare employees).

Counteracting the above flowbacks are the taxes lost on the earnings. The estimated difference between the allowance and would-be earnings for those who would otherwise have worked (assumed to be one-quarter of leave-takers) is:

3 months' leave £66.6m to £97.7m.
6 months' leave £179.3m to £241.5m.

Summing these figures leads to the result in Table 27. It should be noted that the gross cost is assumed to be met from National Insurance, whereas the flowback goes directly to the Exchequer.

Table 27: Summary of gross and net costs for parental leave

	£m		£m
3 months leave:			
gross cost	79.6	–	116.8
tax and benefit flowback	20.0	–	29.8
net cost	59.6	–	87.0
6 months leave:			
gross cost	214.2	–	288.7
tax and benefit flowback	78.7	–	105.2
net cost	135.5	–	183.5

Benefits to children

We have already discussed the prospects that more childcare can reduce poverty amongst children through the effect on household incomes of improving chances for mothers to take paid employment. But there are other potential gains via educational (human capital) effects. These benefits are among the most difficult aspects of pre-school childcare to quantify for a cost-benefit analysis. In the case of disadvantaged children US research has shown significant benefits from investment in pre-school provision, including substantial savings in the cost of remedial provision, unemployment benefit, and prisons. However this research related to a particular educational and family context and we have not attempted to undertake a similar analysis here. But there is a lot of scope for UK childcare to reach disadvantaged families. Children in poor neighbourhoods are the most likely not to have attended any form of group provision outside the family before the age of five. UK research has shown that this can bring significant benefits to children through later educational achievement (Osborn et al).

Benefits to women's pay and career opportunities

Joshi has pioneered calculations of the earnings that women forgo as a result of childcare (see Joshi, 1987). In further work with Davies she has extended these calculations to hypothetical extensions of childcare using European experience (Joshi and Davies,1991b). Lifetime earnings foregone are divided into the effect of years lost, hours lost and pay lost (as compared with a woman without children). For a woman with two children in Britain today she estimates the lifetime earnings foregone at £224,000 (1990 prices), of which £71,900 is due to years lost (eight on average), £74,600 is due to hours lost (14 years working part-time), and £77,280 is due to pay lost (because of loss of experience and because of the lower rates of pay for part-time work.) The loss overall is no less than 57 per cent of total earnings expected between ages 25 and 60 (£393,000).

The models for expansion of childcare in Joshi and Davies are not the same as in this paper but there are similarities. Their two most extensive models are one which permits full-time work while any child was aged one to 15 (ie, two years off for a mother with two children) and another which permits 'long' part-time work in all years with any child aged one to 15 (a Swedish style solution). The simulations are of earnings loss in these two cases of £32,000 and £94,000 respectively. Lower pay rates are responsible for £13,000 and £38,000 respectively of this. Where only two years are spent out of the labour force pay rises in full-time years to some £13,000 per annum in the largely full-time work case and to £12,000 per year in the full-time years of the 'long' part-time case. But in Britain now, when eight years are spent out of the labour force, average maximum salary is around £11,200 per annum. The difference between £11,200 and £12,000 or £13,000 and between a 'lifetime' cost of £77,000 and £38,000 or £13,000 is a measure of the potential boost to women's opportunities from more extensive childcare.

We have estimated the extra earnings from increased labour force participation above (Table 20). This research suggests a further gain because of the effect on rates of pay of reducing the penalty which arises from loss of experience in the labour force. This appears to be worth a third to a half of the participation effects on earnings, which might be added on to those effects. Note that these calculations use human capital models. They predict increases in women's wages but they do not address the further factors which differentiate men's and women's wages - a further difference as much again as that due to childcare (Joshi,1987). However the effect on pay-rates is particularly powerful because it affects lifetime wages, not just those when children are small. If we assume the effect on wages is a third of the participation effects identified in Table 21 then Table 28 shows the further effect on government revenues. (Note: a third is a safer assumption than a half because it is possible that some of the pay lost is in the earnings which we have estimated for years and hours lost.)

Table 28: Extra effect on government revenues from higher lifetime pay for women

		in £ million
1. Model A	1	3,453
	2	1,735
	3	1,625
2. Model B		2,906
3. Model C		769

This lifetime earnings effect even has a further effect - on women's pensions - as Joshi has also explored. (Joshi and Davies,1991a).

Gross and net costs to the Exchequer

Table 29: Summary of costs to the Exchequer

(in £ millions)	Model A	Model B	Model C
Capital costs			
1. training (from table 14)	3,050	4,213	1,600
2. buildings, equipment (from table 15)	1,995.0	3,292.5	1,381.2
Current costs			
3. gross cost (from table 9)	8,136.8	10,986.0	3,693.9
4. government funding share	5,690.3	7,932.3	2,707.7
Revenues			
5. flowback from employment of mothers (from tables 21 and 22)	10,934.4 or 5,680.5 or 5,239.6	9,082	2,481
6. flowback from higher pay for mothers (from table 28)	3,453 or 1,735 or 1,625	2,906	769
7. flowback from childcare employees (from table 26)	2,142.4	2,915.7	1,000.0
8. flowback from parental leave (from table 27)	20.0 or 29.8	20.0 or 29.8	20.0 or 29.8
9. government net current costs (supply side only)*	–8,722.1 or –1,750.3 or –1,194.3	–4,075.7	–562.0

*row 4 minus the sum of rows 5, 6 and 8.

It depends on the macro-economic situation which of the flowbacks is relevant. The flowback from childcare employees is less applicable the nearer is the economy to full employment, but on the other hand then the flowback from the employment of mothers is fully applicable. At other times childcare might add mothers to the labour force with little scope for job expansion - but then childcare employment would help (and anyway reducing supply side constraints will help either to reduce inflation or to sustain expansion longer in the next boom).

Table 29, row 9, shows that in all cases revenue flowbacks exceed the share of current costs assigned to government. This is based on supply side effects only (not allowing for the job creation effect of the programmes). Column 1 of Table 32 shows the internal rate of return to the Treasury. Only in one case, Model C, would this not exceed borrowing costs (the test discount rate), ie only in that case would the increase in Government borrowing be anything more than very temporary. And this is before considering the returns to households.

Benefits to households

Public childcare saves a lot of time in informal care provision, time which we are assuming will to a large extent be turned into productive and income earning work. Some carers will not of course take employment instead, but some value should in principle be attached to extra 'home production' they can achieve instead (Psacharopoulos, 1982). The economies of scale in public as opposed to informal childcare permit this considerable economic gain. Row 2 in table 30 is our estimate of the share to households of the initial value of extra employment by mothers as a result of our three public childcare models. We also noted that this can be considerably enhanced because the shorter breaks in women's careers increases their productiveness and gives a chance for higher incomes (measured in row 3, table 30). The combined effect per household is then shown in Table 31.

Table 30: Benefits and costs to households

(in £ millions)		Model A	Model B	Model C
1. share of childcare costs (table 9)		2,367.0	2,974.0	907.0
2. income gain from employment of mothers (from table 23)		11,204.4	9,221.0	2,055.5
	or	6,682.2		
	or	5,186.0		
3. income gain from higher pay for mothers		3,927.1	3.196.0	743.2
	or	2,386.4		
	or	1,850.0		
4. income gain from childcare employees (from tables 24 & 26)		2,371.8	3,159.4	1,090.7
5. households net income gain (supply side only)*		12,764.5	9,443.0	1,891.7
	or	6,701.6		
	or	4,669.0		

*rows 2 & 3, minus row 1.

Table 31: Average gain for each household with children under 5

		after income tax and NI	after income tax NI and childcare fee
Model A	version 1	£3,780	£3,212
	version 2	£2,078	£1,510
	version 3	£2,325	£1,757
Model B		£2,308	£1,739
Model C		£608	£456

This shows the average gain per household, whether affected or not by the childcare programme. Calculated from estimated total figures like Table 23, but for mothers of under fives and including higher pay from the skill effect.

The high and positive net income gains (row 5, Table 30 and column 2, Table 31) very much reinforce the positive returns to the Exchequer shown in Table 29. They are presented without including the additional income gains from the job creation aspect of childcare (row 4 of Table 30), because that will not necessarily be an overall gain. The internal rates of return when returns to households are added to returns to the Treasury are shown in Table 32, column 2.

We have also discussed benefits to children from a childcare programme. Over a million children under five are currently in poverty - at least a half would be brought out of poverty if public childcare enabled their mothers to work. There is also evidence of educational benefits (including to incomes when adults) for disadvantaged children in public childcare.

Table 32: Internal rate of return calculations

(Based on benefits via employment of mothers only)

		Return to Treasury	Social cost-benefit return
Model A	version 1	51%	84%
	version 2	13%	44%
	version 3	7%	32%
Model B		21%	50%
Model C		5%	24%

Assumptions

1. Training and capital costs spread over years 1-10 in ten equal parts.
2. Current costs accrue from year 4, beginning with 1/10 final size, then rising steadily to reach full size from year 13.
3. Employment of mothers expands from year 4 and reaches full size from year 13.
4. Skill effect (higher pay for mothers) is from year 11, with no phasing in.
5. Internal rate of return calculated on net benefits to year 20.

Conclusion

Public childcare programmes are shown as a good investment for the economy and society. The predicted GDP gain is the sum of the net gains to the Treasury and households, plus the effects on the corporate sector (which are very difficult to predict but are unlikely to be negative). The largest rate of return gain is for a Danish programme with Danish employment rates. But when the three Models use a similar basis for prediction of the employment effect, rates of return are in order of size (Model B gives the greatest return, followed by Model A3 and then Model C). This seems to be because the 'deadweight' effect is proportionately smaller, the bigger the programme. This result favouring bigger programmes applies as long as expansion of child-care is within the range where the mothers concerned want to take employment.

BIBLIOGRAPHY

Adam Smith Institute (1989), *Mind the Children*, London, Adam Smith Institute

Bell, C; McKee, L & Priestly, K (1983), *Fathers, Childbirth and Work*, EOC Manchester

Bone, M (1977), *Pre-school Children and the Need for Daycare*, HMSO, London

Bradshaw, J, Millar, J (1991), *Lone Parent Families in the UK*, HMSO

Bansbury, L (forthcoming) *Escaping from Dependency: Welfare Strategies for Working Parents*, IPPR, London

Brennan, D and Stonehouse, A in Cochran, M (ed) (forthcoming) op cit, *Australia*

Brown, J (1987), *In Search of a Policy – the Rationale for Social Security Provision for One Parent Families*, NCOPF, London

C.A.G. Consultants (1988), *Economic Development for the People of Norwich*, City of Norwich

Cass, B (1990), *Why Public Investment in Childcare Matters: Econo mic and Social Issues*. Address presented at Golden Jubilee of Lady Gowrie Child Centre

CEC (1990, a), Women in Europe, *Childcare in Europe, 1985-1990*, CEC

CEC (1990, b), Families and Policies: Evaluations and Trends 1988-1989, CEC

CEC (1990, c), *Third Equal Opportunities Action Programme* 1991-5, COM90 44913, CEC

CEC (1991), *Final Report on the Second European Poverty Programme*, 1985-1989 , CEC

Central Statistical Office (1987), *Family Expenditure Survey*

Central Statistical Office (1991), *Social Trends*

CIPFA (1989-90) *Personal Social Service Statistics*, CIPFA, London

Cochran, M (ed) (forthcoming), *International Handbook of Daycare Policy and Programmes*, Greenwood Press, New York

Cohen, B in Cochran, M (ed) (forthcoming), op cit, *United Kingdom*

Cohen, B (1989), *Structural Funding in Childcare: Current Funding Applications and Policy Implications*, CEC, V/2267/18-EN

Cohen, B (1990), *Caring for Children: The 1990 Report*, Family Policy Studies Centre

Coote, A *et al* (1990) *The Family Way*, Social Policy Paper No.1, IPPR, London

Daniel, W W (1990), *Maternity Rights, The Experience of Women*, Policy Studies Institute, London

Dept. of Employment (1989), Results from Labour Force Survey, Spring 1989, *Employment Gazette*

Dept. of Employment (1990), *New Earnings Survey*

Dept. of Health (1989, a), *An Introduction to the Children Act*, HMSO, London

Dept. Of Health (1989, b), *Children's Day Care Facilities at 31.3.88*, HMSO, London

Dept. of Health (1991), *The Children Act 1989:* Guidance and Regulation Vol.2. Family Support, Daycare and Educational Provision for Young Children. HMSO, London

DES (1986), *Statistics of Education: Teachers in Service. England & Wales*, HMSO, London

DES (1989), *Statistical Bulletin*, HMSO, London

DES (1990), *Education Statistics for UK*, HMSO, London

DSS (1990), *Households below Average Income 1981-1987*. Govt. Statistical Service, HMSO, London

EC Childcare Network (1990, a), *Childcare Needs of Rural Families*, CEG, V/1732/90-EN

EC Childcare Network (1990, b), *Men as Carers for Children*, CEC, V/1731/90-EN

EC Childcare Network (1990, c), *Childcare Workers with Children Under Four*, CEC, V/1730/90-EN

EC Childcare Network (1990, d), *Quality in Childcare Services*, CEC, V/1730/90-EN

Equal Opportunities Commission (1990), *The Key to Real Choice and Action Plan for Childcare*, EOC, Manchester

Equal Opportunities Commission (1991), *Women and Men*, EOC, Manchester

Elliott, F R (1978), Occupational Commitments and Paternal Deprivation. *Childcare, Health and Development ,4*

Family Policy Studies Centre (1991) *Family Policy Bulletin*, March, FPSC , London

Finch, J (1989), *Family Obligations, Social Changes*, Polity Press, London

Garland, C and White, S (1980), *Children and Day Nurseries*, Grant & MacIntyre, London

Holtermann, S (1986), *The Costs of Implementing Parental Leave in Great Britain*, EOC, Manchester

House of Commons Select Committee (1988/89), *Education Provision for the Under Fives*, HMSO, London

Industrial Relations Review and Report (1989, a), *Report 439*, May, London

Industrial Relations Review and Report (1989, b), *Report 442*, June, London

Joshi, H, in Glendinning, C & Millar, J (1987), The Cost of Caring, *Women and Poverty in Britain*, Wheatsheaf, Brighton

Joshi, H & Davies, H (1991, a), *The Pension Consequences of Divorce*, CEPR Discussion Paper 550, London

Joshi, H & Davies, H (1991, b), *Childcare Institutions in Europe and Mothers' Foregone Earnings*, Paper for SPE91 Conference, Pisa

Kids Clubs Network (1991, a), Newsletter, London

Kids Clubs Network (1990, b), *A Patchwork of Provision*, London

Kiernan, K & Wicks, M (1991), *Family Change and Future Policy*, Family Policies Study Centre, London

Kilmurray, A & Bradley, C (1989), *Rural Women in South Armagh: Needs and Aspirations*, Rural Action Projects, Derry

Langstad, O & Sommer, D. in Cochran, M (ed) (forthcoming) op cit, *Changing Socialisation Patterns, Child Policies and Programmes in Contemporary Denmark.*

Lister, R (1990), *The Exclusive Society. Citizenship and the Poor*, CPAG, London

Mann, L (1991), *Women Returners to the Labour Market in Ross and Cromarty*, Ross and Cromarty District

Martin, J and Roberts, C (1984), *Women and Employment A Lifetime Perspective*, HMSO, London

May, H (1990), *From a Floor to a Drawer*, Paper for Second Education Policy Conference, August, Wellington, New Zealand

Mayall, B & Petrie, P (1983), *Childminding and Day Nurseries: What Kind of Care?*, Heinemann Educational, London

McRae, S & Daniel, W (1991), *Maternity Rights – the Experience of Women and Employers*, Policy Studies Institute, London

Melhuish & Moss (1990) *Daycare for Young Children: International Perspectives. Policy and Research in Five Countries*, Routledge, London

Metcalf, H and Leighton, P (1989), *The Under-Utilisation of Women in the Labour Market*, EOC/Institute of Manpower Studies, Manchester

Ministry of Community and Social Services, Ontario (1988), *New Directions for Childcare*, Queen's Printer for Ontario

Moss, P (1988), *Childcare and Equality of Opportunity*, CEC

Moss, P (1989), The Indirect Costs of Parenthood. A Neglected Issue in Social Policy, *Critical Social Policy*

Musatti, J (1990), *The Daily Life of Toddlers in Italy*, unpublished paper presented at conference organised by the Centre for Research and Child Development, Edinburgh University, September 1990

National Child Care Staffing Study (1990), *Who Cares? Child Care Teachers and the Quality of Care in America*, Childcare Employee Project, USA

Ontario Coalition for Better Childcare (1991), *Childcare Challenge*, Spring, vol 8 no 5, Ontario

OPCS (1988), *General Household Survey*

OPCS (1989), *Population Projections 1987-2027*

Oppenheim, C (1990), *Poverty – The Facts*, CPAG, London

Osborn, A, Butler, A, & Morris A, (1984) *The Social Life of Britain's Five Year Old*, Routledge & Kegan Paul, London

Osborne, A and Milbank, J (1987), *The Effects of Early Education. A Report from the Child Health and Education Survey*, OUP, Oxford

Owen, R (1813), *A New View of Society or Essays on the Principles of Formation of the Human Character and the Application of the Principle to Practice*, Cadell & Davies, London

Owen, R (1972), *Robert Owen at New Lanark, two booklets and one pamphlet 1824-1838*, Arno Press, New York

Penn, H (forthcoming), *The Rise of Private Nurseries*

Petrie, P and Logan, P (1986), *After School and in the Holidays: the Responsibility of Looking After School Children*, TCRU, London

Pfeffer, N, Coote, A, *Is Quality Good for You?*, IPPR, 1991

Pollock, A (1991), *Childcare and Equal Opportunities*, Working Document of the Committee on Women's Rights, European Parliament, PE 1465. 438

Psacharopoulos, G (1982), The Economics of Early Childhood Education and Daycare, *International Review of Education*

Scott, G (1989), *Families and Under-Fives in Strathclyde*, Strathclyde Regional Council, Glasgow

SCAFA, Scottish Child and Family Alliance (1991), *Childcare in Rural Communities* – Scotland in Europe, HMSO London

Scottish Development Agency (1989), *Developing Nurseries in Glasgow*

Schaffer, H R (1990), *Making Decisions about Children – Psychological Questions and Answers*, Blackwell, Oxford

Simpson, R, (1986) The Cost of Childcare Services in *Childcare and Equal Opportunities*, EOC, Manchester

Smith, A (forthcoming) Early Childhood Educare in New Zealand in 1990: Winds of Change, in *International Handbook of Early Childhood Education*

Sorrentino, C (1990), The Changing Family in International Perspective, *Monthly Labour Review*, March

Statham, J *et al* (1990), *Playgroups in a Changing World*, HMSO, London

Summerfield, P (1984), *Women Workers in the 2nd World War*, Croom Helm, London

Thomas Coram Research Unit (1990), unpublished data

Townson, M (1986), *The Costs and Benefits of a National Child Care System for Canada*, Canadian Day Care Advocacy Association

Weikart, D (1982), *The Cost Effectiveness of High Quality Early Education Programmes*, High/Scope Educational Foundation

Woodhead, M (1986) Pre-school Education has Long-term Effects: But can they be Generalised?, *Oxford Review of Education*

Working for Childcare (1991), *Childcare in the Balance*, Working for Childcare, London

Whittinham, V (1991), *Full Marks for Trying: A Survey of Childcare Providers*, Daycare Trust

IPPR Welfare Series, 1991/92

STRATEGIES FOR A MODERN WELFARE SYSTEM

This series is based on a major IPPR project, directed by Anna Coote, which aims to develop a new agenda for welfare, suited to the needs and conditions of the 1990s and beyond. The project is supported by the Joseph Rowntree Foundation, Leeds City Council, the Calouste Gulbenkian Foundation and King Edward's Hospital Fund for London, with additional grants from the Forbes Trust and the Nuffield Foundation.

Meeting Needs in the 1990s
The future of public service and the challenge for trade unions
Bill Callaghan, Anna Coote, Geoffrey Hulme, John Stewart
Published in association with the TUC. The authors examine the main issues confronting public services; they urge unions to abandon defensive positions adopted during the 1980s and take a 'bold and innovative stance' in order to meet the challenges of the 1990s and improve the quality of services. (Price £7.50)

Health Before Health Care
David Harrison, David J. Hunter, Ian Johnston, Nick Nicholson, Colin Thunhurst, Gerald Wistow
A practical new approach to health policy which seeks to promote better health for the nation as a whole. The authors examine the main issues confronting public services; they urge unions to abandon defensive positions adopted during the 1980s and take a 'bold and innovative stance' in order to meet the challenges of the 1990s and improve the quality of services. (Price: £7.50)

Is Quality Good for You?
A critical review of quality assurance in welfare services
Naomi Pfeffer and Anna Coote
What lies behind the widespread interest in promoting 'quality' in the public sector? the authors examine current approaches to quality assurance in welfare services and ask how far they serve or damage the interests of the public as customers and as citizens. (Price: £10.00)

Childcare in a Modern Welfare System
Towards a new national policy
Bronwen Cohen and Neil Fraser
The authors argue that childcare should be integral to a modern welfare system and demonstrate that a new national childcare policy will pay substantial social and economic dividends. They set out practical proposals for flexible and responsive childcare services. (Price: £10.00)

Equal Rights for Disabled People
The case for a new law
Ian Bynoe, Mike Oliver, Colin Barnes
Definitive proposals for enacting legislation to outlaw discrimination on grounds of disability. (Price: £5.00)

Citizens' Rights in Modern Welfare System
Edited by Anna Coote
A major collection of papers: develops a philosophical and practical framework for rights to health and social services. Authors include Raymond Plant, Denis Galligan, Norman Lews, Priscilla Alderson, Wendy Thompson, Jonathan Montgomery, Nina Biehal, Nick Doyle, Tessa Harding. (Price: £10.00) *Forthcoming.*

Escaping from Dependency: W elfare strategies for working parents
Lynda Bransbury
How can social security, taxation, labour market strategies and local services best enable people to combine paid employment and parenthood? The author examines policies in other European countries and sets out a new policy agenda. (Price: £10.00) *Forthcoming.*

Needs in Leeds
Ian Sanderson, Janie Percy-Smith, Ian Gough, Jo Cutter
Report and assessment of Britain's first audit of welfare needs. (Price: £10.00)

Welfare Beyond the State
Anna Coote and Nicholas Deakin
What should be the role of voluntary organisations, and how should self-help and mutual aid feature in a modern welfare system? (Price £7.50) *Forthcoming.*

IPPR WELFARE SERIES: special subscription rate, £50
Includes all titles listed above. Orders to IPPR, 30-32 Southampton Street, London WC2E 7RA. Cheques payable to IPPR.